Violent Deaths in the Bible

Violent Deaths in the Bible

*Eighteen Shocking Tales of Judgment
and Redemption*

JONAH HADDAD

WIPF & STOCK · Eugene, Oregon

VIOLENT DEATHS IN THE BIBLE
Eighteen Shocking Tales of Judgment and Redemption

Wipf & Stock
An Imprint of Wipf and Stock Publishers
199 W. 8th Ave., Suite 3
Eugene, OR 97401

www.wipfandstock.com

PAPERBACK ISBN: 979-8-3852-1211-8
HARDCOVER ISBN: 979-8-3852-1212-5
EBOOK ISBN: 979-8-3852-1213-2

VERSION NUMBER 05/16/24

For my wife Amy
Thank you for your patience
and support

I love you

Contents

Illustration Credits

Mark Bell: "Shanked in the Gut," "Defenestration, Pulverization, and Mastication," "Strange Fire," "Valley of Slaughter," "Rotten Bowels," "Dismembered Concubine," "Eaten by Worms," "Slain by the Spirit," "Grisly Suicide," "Death by Preaching," "Damnation in Flame," and "Skull and Crossbones."

John Mason: "Curse of Bears," "Pillar of Salt," "Witches, Ghosts, and Bloody Death," "Gruesome Annihilation," "Severed Head," "Cruel Stonework," and "Blood-Soaked Crucifix."

Introduction

IRREVERENT AND PROFANE CONTENT litter the pages of Scripture. Stories of stabbing, beheading, dismemberment, defenestration, trampling, burning, and mauling are commonplace. The Bible can appear almost irreligious. Sometimes it's just plain gross. Many passages can seem unworthy of making an appearance in church. Gaping wounds and festering sores don't draw crowds. Rotting corpses fair no better. The violence of the Bible is something many would no doubt prefer to gloss over and ignore. It gets in the way of beauty, grace, and love. It's unaesthetic. It's counterproductive. It's shocking and distracting from the glorious gospel of salvation. Or is it?

Everything in the Bible is there for a reason. In the last verse of his gospel account, the apostle John says: "Now there are also many other things that Jesus did. Were every one of them to be written, I suppose that the world itself could not contain the books that would be written" (John 21:25). This is a curious statement. John is telling us that God could have inspired the biblical writers to add so much more to our Bibles. God could have said anything he wanted, providing myriad stories of faith and miracles to inspire us. Instead, he saw fit to intermingle ugliness with beauty, death with life. He chose to tell us something about painful sores, festering wounds, and loathsome heaps of gore and viscera.

Violence is pivotal to the overall message of Scripture. There, at the center of the story—at the center of all time and space—is the brutal, bloody cross of Jesus Christ. The violence of the Bible can't be ignored. It can't be swept under the rug. Violence is there whether we like it or not. Sanitizing it might make it more palatable. Distilling it might make it go down more smoothly. But covering it up won't make it go away. In fact, when we fail to confront the violence of the Bible, we miss out on a complete and robust picture of theological anthropology—the divine perspective of humans as created, fallen, and redeemed beings. God has reminded us that we are disordered people who live in a disordered world, replete with every sin and shameful behavior imaginable. We have done violence to each other. We have done violence to the Son of God. Likewise, even God himself has done violence when necessary.

With all this in mind, I realize writing a book about violence in the Bible is a risky endeavor. The subject matter must be handled with care. To treat the violence of Scripture with lofty academic disdain, as a purely objective observer, doesn't seem to do justice to the topic. To treat violence with the base, crass irreverence so fitting the topic would likewise require overstepping the tone that Scripture itself often takes. In the process of mapping out, researching and writing this project, there were times I would casually mention my work to friends and colleagues. Rarely did the project elicit an initial positive response. The reaction was always cautious: "Hmm, I'm not sure about that. It sounds unique. It sounds edgy. Would people read that?" Other times, the response was a simple smile and a polite acknowledgement: "That could be interesting. Let me know how it goes."

These wise men and women certainly recognized the risk. Serious subjects require serious treatment. Yet, irreverent themes might need some irreverent elaboration. A unique topic demands a unique approach. Be funny. Be winsome. Be vulgar. But be careful. It's a perilous venture—too impious for churchgoers, and too Christian for the unchurched. Violence is no laughing matter. Death is a somber, sobering thing. So, good luck.

What you'll find in the following pages is my attempt to do my best at taking the lesson of each violent episode seriously, while not taking myself too seriously. I invite you to enjoy the content of this book, and maybe even laugh, cringe, or question at times. I also invite you into serious self-examination as you read and reflect on each episode. My disclaimer is this: Serious biblical scholars will likely find this book unconventional, if not unhelpful as a scholarly commentary. I admit that many bigger theological points and motifs were left untouched. That's fine with me. This book is not intended to be a definitive account of the nuance of each and every difficult question that arises in the biblical text. In fact, I readily acknowledge that in these arenas, I don't quite delve far enough into grammar, syntax, and historical and theological concerns to satisfy the academic commentator. On the contrary, casual readers who are willing to place one foot into the slightly off-color realm of R-rated Bible stories with an open mind and desire to grow in familiarity with Scripture, might find this book useful as a devotional and pastoral study.

This book is for people who've rarely paused to fathom the grotesque aesthetic of biblical violence. My hope is that this book will settle nicely into the hands of people who don't generally take time to read anything theological—people who rarely find excitement in biblical reflections. It might even settle nicely into the hands of those who read too many heavy-duty analytic theological books and just need something a little lighter to bring them back down to the quotidian and visceral. I'd like to think of this book as a little more than mere coffee table fodder or bathroom reading. This book is commentary. It's also devotional. It's playful. It's pastoral. I hope you will chuckle. I hope you will learn. I would be loath to see you remain unchanged by these reflections on the word of God and what the word means for us today.

My content cannot be divorced from my convictions. I write as a biblically minded Protestant Christian in the evangelical tradition, who holds the following assumptions: First, I take all Scripture to be breathed out by God (2 Tim 3:16). These are not mere human stories. They are in the Bible because God put them there. I stand squarely in the camp of biblical scholars and theologians who hold fast to the authority, inspiration, and inerrancy of Scripture. Scholars, like D.A Carson and John Frame, have provided compelling defenses of the Bible's divine qualities.[1] Theologians, like Wayne Grudem, have aptly reminded us that "if the Bible cannot be trusted, then God himself cannot be trusted.[2] Of course, there will always be questions about the interface between divine and human action in the actual writing of the biblical text. There will be questions about the creation of the biblical canon. There will be questions about putative contradictions in the biblical text. I don't intend to answer those questions here. I will only say this much: Scripture is inspired by God, persevered by God, and authoritative in all it says.

Second, I would argue that all Scripture is instructive. The stories of violence that seem to mar the pages of Scripture are there for a reason, and if we take the time to study them, there are lessons for us to learn. Even stories that verge on excessive brevity and ambiguity should not be ignored. The Bible is teaching us something important about God and about ourselves. We need to do the hard work of reading, thinking, praying, and seeking God as Scripture speaks to us. Some questions that should be at the forefront of our study of violent death in the Bible are: Why is

1. See Carson, *Enduring Authority* and Frame, *Doctrine of the Word*.

2. Grudem, *Christian Beliefs*, 5.

this story here? and What might this story teach me about theology (God), anthropology (humans), hamartiology (sin), Christology (Christ), and soteriology (salvation)?

Finally, I believe that all Scripture aims us toward the cross of Jesus Christ. That is not to say that all Scripture directly references the cross of Christ. But the Bible has been given to us that we might grow in our understanding of God's overall work through the unfolding of the story of creation, fall, redemption, and glorification. The Bible takes us on a journey to the cross, because without the death and resurrection of Jesus Christ, we would be without hope. Though sometimes shocking, usually ugly, and always instructive, the violent episodes of the Bible culminate at the cross where Jesus suffered and died on behalf of a fallen human race. Excluding the redemptive work of Christ at the cross, the Bible would be little more than a moral code book filled with interesting bedtime stories.

Violent Deaths in the Bible will take you places your Sunday school picture Bible refuses to go. It will offend you with stories not fit for the shelves of the "inspiration" section of the local Christian bookstore. It will shock you even as it guides you to the most meaningful death of all—the death of Jesus on the cross. With this, I invite you to join me in exploring the stories you didn't learn in Sunday school.

The Old Testament

1

Curse of Bears — 2 Kings 2

"He went up from there to Bethel, and while he was going up on the way, some small boys came out of the city and jeered at him, saying, 'Go up, you baldhead! Go up, you baldhead!' And he turned around, and when he saw them, he cursed them in the name of the Lord. And two she-bears came out of the woods and tore forty-two of the boys."

—2 KINGS 2:23–24

MOCKING GOD AND HIS word could get a person mauled by bears. At least this happened once in Elisha's day. Bears technically belong to the order *carnivora*. Practically, however, they are omnivores. Their diet consists of berries, leaves, grasses, insects, fish, small animals, and carrion. They also like porridge, pizza, and microwave dinners when they can get them. And garbage. From time to time, I catch a glimpse of a black bear from my Colorado home in the early morning hours as it returns to its lair after a night of rifling through the neighbor's trash bin. Bears are crepuscular and nocturnal hunters, preferring the twilight hours and the cover of darkness. I consider myself lucky whenever I see one.

The claws of a black bear are roughly two inches in length. Grizzly claws are closer to four inches. Bear claws of any size are intimidating when you consider the powerful limbs to which they are attached. Bear teeth are another matter entirely. Beneath their fluffy exterior bears are heavily muscled, ferocious beasts that will tear out your throat with one swipe of their paw, or so literature and overactive imaginations might say.

Aggression toward humans is rare among members of the family of *Ursidae* (their scientific name). Occasionally, someone runs in to a protective mother bear. Nineteenth century trapper and frontiersman, Hugh Glass, famously survived a brutal grizzly bear mauling that left him with a broken leg, a punctured throat, a torn scalp, and numerous deep lacerations, among other wounds.[1] Though Glass allegedly killed the bear that battered him, the bear seems to have gotten the better end of the exchange, because Glass's buddies decided he wasn't worth mending. The two men threw his body in a shallow grave and took off, leaving him to die a slow agonizing death. Somehow, perhaps by sheer force of will, Glass regained enough strength to dig himself out of his grave, dust himself off, bind his wounds and crawl, limp, and stagger his way across 250 miles of rugged American frontier to Fort Kiowa in present day South Dakota. His survival was nothing short of a miracle (that is, in the non-biblical sense of miracle, where circumstances just seem to come together in a person's favor). Maybe Glass was just lucky.

The "Grizzly Man," Timothy Treadwell, was not so lucky.[2] In 2003, the self-proclaimed protector and friend of grizzlies was mauled to death along with his girlfriend in Alaska. Apparently when bears can't get their paws on a nice gravlax or fillet mignon, they settle for raw human. While black bears usually run from humans, grizzlies do not. They think they're at the top of the North American food chain. Grizzlies do whatever they feel like doing. If they want to kill, they kill. And they probably don't even feel bad about mauling people to death either. I recently heard a helpful anecdote for dealing with various kinds of bear attacks: If it's black, fight back; If it's brown, lay down; If it's white, goodnight. Yes, polar bears can be a problem for humans, too.

In any case, stories of bear attacks abound, but my all-time favorite is found in 2 Kings. Here we find the prophet Elisha on his way to Bethel, a town north of Jerusalem, when he is surrounded by young hecklers—a gang of street miscreants who think his male pattern receding hairline is somehow funny.[3] The moral of the story, at first blush, is this: Don't laugh

---

1. See Myers, *Saga of Hugh Glass.*

2. See the 2005 documentary *Grizzly Man.*

3. I've heard it speculated that references to Elisha's baldness cannot refer to a lack of hair on his head, since men in the ancient near East would not have traveled with

at other people's baldness. It can be dangerous to your health. Some bald men are not to be trifled with; think Bruce Willis, Dwayne Johnson, and Jason Statham. In his prime, Jesse the Body was no joke either. The list goes on. But no list of bald tough guys is complete without the prophet Elisha. Though this man of God probably wouldn't pummel you in the face or tear your arm off and beat you with it, he might just miraculously send down a rogue bear to sucker punch you in the throat with its gnarly clawed bear fist.

In reading 2 Kings 2, I like to picture Elisha as a wild-eyed, robed, and bearded wizardly man standing on a rock outcropping with black clouds swirling overhead while sharp-fanged mutant children encroach for the kill. Gesturing in their direction with a crazed look, the prophet shoots bears from spell-bound hands and obliterates the threat.

While bald-shaming, capricious fits of vengeance, and bear carnage seem to be at the center of this story, we might need to slow down and take another look. There's a little more going on here than first meets the eye. If all Scripture is God-breathed and useful to our fundamental understanding of theology (who God is), anthropology (who humans are), and how the two relate in judgment and redemption, it is crucial to ask why 2 Kings 2:23–24 happened in the first place, and why the Spirit inspired the author of Kings to include it.

If we don't do our hermeneutical and exegetical homework, and if we fail to ask a few questions of observation and interpretation, we end up jumping immediately to the most obvious and immediate application, no matter how wrong that application might be: Some kids mocked God's anointed prophet and they were punished for it; therefore, don't mock pastors, elders, or Sunday school teachers, or you might regret it. Pastors, after all, are easy to mock. They set themselves up. Bad jokes, dated clothing, and a propensity to turn the other cheek make them an easy target of mockery and derision. Hipster tattooed pastors with edgy sermons and too much styling gel don't fare much better. The best defense these poor men of God have at their disposal is the greatest trump card of all time, the ability to call down a curse of she-bears on unsuspecting parishioners. But that can't be the main takeaway here. Can it?

---

their heads uncovered, making the condition of Elisha's follicle situation unknown to the hecklers. Honestly, what else could it be referring to? I don't really buy it. Let's be honest. The guy was probably bald.

GOD WILL NOT BE MOCKED

So, what's really going on in this story? Have a group of schoolboys been gruesomely dismembered by a divinely sanctioned bear-attack simply because they made a couple of jests at a silly bald man who was walking by their playground? To suggest as much would be to miss some key elements of the story.

The Hebrew word *na'ar* is often rendered "boy" or "young man" in English. It can also refer to a servant, as in Genesis 22:3, where Abraham takes his young men with him as he goes off to make a sacrifice to God. *Na'ar* can refer to an armor-bearer, as in Judges 9:54, where Abimelek tells his young man to draw his sword and finish him after he has been mortally wounded. Furthermore, *na'ar* can be used to signify young men associated with the priesthood, as in the account of Eli's sons in 1 Samuel 2. The point here is to slow down and not assume the victims of the bear attack in 2 Kings are innocent, though unwise, school children.

On the other hand, context often gives us some indication of age and station in life. The Scripture references mentioned above give us some indicators that would place the *na'ar* in question within a context of servant, armor bearer, or priest. The context of 2 Kings 2 likewise gives us some clues. Elisha is on his way to Bethel, a town associated with Jeraboam's golden calves (1 Kgs 12). Bethel was also located in a region of Israel that was rife with Baal and Asherah worship during the reign of King Ahab and Queen Jezebel, who ruled around the time of Elisha's tenure as a prophet.

Could it be that the young men who came out to jeer were defenders of idolatrous worship? Though the text is not explicit on this, it seems a reasonable assumption. Perhaps their insults, "Go up, you baldhead," were intended to harken back to Elisha's predecessor Elijah. The latter had been taken up to heaven in a fiery chariot, as recounted in the earlier part of 2 Kings 2. It seems perfectly fair to suggest that these young men were enemies of God and his divinely appointed prophets. To assume the boys mentioned in the passage are silly, if not unruly, school children doesn't seem to fit the severity of the punishment. But again, we can't know for sure since the biblical text gives no precision to their age. The most natural reading of the text suggests that these were recalcitrant youths.

And what of the she-bears? The bears in question here were likely Syrian brown bears (*ursus arctos syriacus*), whose territory has varied historically throughout various Middle Eastern countries. I've heard it surmised that since the text says nothing of death and blood, these bears served only to frighten the boys. After all, mauling and butchering narratives don't fit well in our politically correct churches, where peace-loving, hippy Jesuses greet parishioners with high-fives and fist-bumps. So, these must have been nice bears—trained Russian circus bears, declawed, and well-fed. These were bears along the lines of Smokey and Yogi. They walked out of the woods to give a brief lesson to the children on the danger of forest fires, unattended picnics, and bullying. Then they sang a song and danced back into the forest. Never mind that the Hebrew word translated "to tear" in 2 Kings 2:24 also translates "to cleave" and "to split." The reality is, this was no Winnie the Pooh. Nor were these the Care Bears. These were the "Tear Bears." These bears were hardened psychopathic killers jacked up on cocaine.

We need to be careful not to sanitize the story, diminishing the severity of the punishment by making the boys older and meaner, and the bears gentler and kinder. We tell ourselves the boys were a mob of devil-worshippers, and the bears were cartoonish mascots. We tell ourselves that the text only says the bears "tore" the boys. That could mean they lightly batted them around in their paws. This rendering makes the story easier to digest but it doesn't make for a natural and honest reading of the text. If these boys were defenders of idolatry and Baal worship, what's to say that a perfect and holy God would not strike them in vengeance? Second Kings 2:23–24 is a story of carnage, the aftermath of which would have likely included a heap of severed limbs, gore, and bloodied ribcages sticking up from pools of gooey viscera.

It is unlikely the boys in question acted in ignorance. They knew who Elisha was and they neither respected him nor the God he represented. They weren't just insulting his glistening scalp; they were rejecting the very God who had chosen Elisha to be his servant. An insult on the carrier of the message is as good as a rejection of the one who wrote the message—in this case YHWH, the creator God who delivered Israel out of the bonds of slavery in Egypt and had graciously given them his law and covenant promise. Retributive justice in the Old Testament speaks to the severity of mocking God and those who convey his revealed word (Deut 7:10; 18:19). The curse called down by Elisha is in keeping with the words of God spoken in Leviticus 26:21–2:

> Then if you walk contrary to me and will not listen to me, I will continue striking you, sevenfold for your sins. And I will let loose the wild beasts against you, which shall bereave you of your

children and destroy your livestock and make you few in number, so that your roads shall be deserted.

Outright rejection of God's covenant of salvation merits a visit from the "covenant bears."[4] The forty-two young men who mocked Elisha had doomed themselves. Their blood was on their own heads. It seems fair to suggest that they knowingly cursed themselves by giving their allegiance to something other than the true God. But God will not be mocked (Gal 6:7). Every knee will bow, and every tongue confess the lordship of the one and only true God (Phil 2:10–11). As we see in the story of Elisha and the she-bears, sometimes God judges rebellion in the moment. Other times he saves it for eternity. Either way, all people will be judged with equity by the perfect judge (2 Cor 5:10).

What we witness in 2 Kings 2 is a street brawl that got out of hand. What we don't see behind the scenes was the spiritual battle that transpired between God and his enemies. This was not a mere back-alley Jets-and-Sharks-style dance-fight. This wasn't even about Elisha and his bear thugs against the notorious na'ar brothers. This was about God and his holy perfections being mocked and rejected by people who should have known better.

FROM MOCKERY TO REVERENCE

When the gospel is preached and the truth is spoken in love, some will ignore it, others will repudiate it, and still others will revile it with the hardest of hearts. When Jesus is proclaimed as a friend of sinners and lover of the lost, who freely gave his life for them as a ransom, some will respond to him in hatred. They might even gladly scorn his love and heap insults on his grace. And if people reject God in his grace and mercy toward them, how much more will they reject him in his judgment of their evil.

Human nature drives us to blame the source of justice for our crimes. We rebel against God and then blame him when he gives us a just recompense for our rebellion. We invite God's judgment when we sin against him, then we shake our fists at him when he gives us what we ask for. In a way, God just can't seem to win with human beings. We hate him because we hate him. Rebellion is our natural default setting.

4. Davis, *2 Kings*, 39.

We think God's grace is too good to be true. So, we mock it. His judgment is too harsh to be merited. So, we mock that too. No biblical account captures this better than the account of the crucifixion of Jesus (Matt 27:27–44 and Luke 23:26–43). They robed him in a scarlet robe and crowned him with thorns. They knelt before him and mocked him saying, "hail, king of the Jews." They beat him and heaped insults on him. "You who saved others, save yourself," they scoffed. And for what? For healing the sick, and preaching the truth? For warning people of the coming judgment? For offering salvation to those who clearly couldn't save themselves?

Jesus said in Matthew 5:11–12:

> Blessed are you when others revile you and persecute you and utter all kinds of evil against you falsely on my account. Rejoice and be glad, for your reward is great in heaven, for so they persecuted the prophets who were before you.

The point here is that just as Jesus was mocked, so too will his followers be mocked. Mockery is a promise. So, my suggestion to Christians is this: If you're going to be mocked, be mocked for the right reasons. Be mocked for being a child of God, and for doing the things of God. Don't be mocked for being a jerk. Elisha was mocked primarily for his obedience to God's call on his life. He simply answered the call and did the things God had asked him to do. The mocking he received for being bald was likely the best thing his adversaries could come up with, knowing they had no real argument against Elisha and his God. The youths of Bethel had no argument. Elisha was mocked because he spoke the truth and lived in the truth of the true and living God. He wasn't mocked for rudely forcing conversions, or for using his power to manipulate people. He wasn't mocked for making a big political stink and aligning himself behind corrupt legislators. Elisha didn't pick a fight, or claim that he was better than everyone else, simply because he was a prophet of the Most High God. Elisha's only offense to the young men in the story, so far as I can tell, was that of obedience to God and faithful transmission of God's word.

Granted, at times God has inspired a prophet to call down judgment on sinners. The example of Elisha and the bears is one such case. These accounts are few and far between. God inspires such events according to his perfect will. Remember, you are not Elisha. Don't try this at home. Rather, when people despise you, count yourself blessed. He might send them another chance. He might send them bears. Either way, no matter how he chooses to act, God will probably ask you to endure hardship for his sake.

Followers of Christ and speakers of truth will be scorned. But do not be ignorant of your own mockeries against God. Many self-proclaimed believers in God might just unwittingly find themselves in the company of the forty-two youths. How do we mock God and his prophets, you ask? Simple. By diminishing the authority of his word. By making it too human. By forgetting that though human hands penned the words of Scripture, those hands were divinely guided to say exactly what God wanted said. We join the ranks of the young men of Bethel when we declare: "I don't like what Paul says about that subject; I think John was on drugs when he wrote that; poor Moses embellished that story to make himself look good." Or, more subtly, we ask ourselves, "did God really mean what he said?" "Surely God is not so out of touch as to reveal such primitive concepts." We who turn up our noses with a glint of arrogance in our eyes: Be warned. Minimizing the authority of God's instruction is mockery. If all Scripture is breathed out by God, then we don't get to decide what we like and dislike (2 Tim 3:16).

Just remember, those who mock God have cursed themselves. They will be judged according to their deeds. But worse than dismemberment by way of bear attack, those who reject God will face an eternity of punishment (Rev 20:11–15). The good news is that they might also be saved by turning to Christ in repentance. Jesus became a curse on our behalf that we might no longer live under the curse (Gal 3:13). In other words, he bore our sin and its consequences. He took what was rightfully ours (sin and death) and gave us what is rightfully his (righteousness and life), if by faith we receive his gift of grace.

STUDY QUESTIONS

1. Have you ever unfairly ridiculed anyone (even in your mind/heart)? What were the consequences?

2. Read 1 Kings 19:19–21 and 2 Kings 2:1–22. Who is Elisha according to this account?

3. What does the story of Elisha and the bears (2 Kgs 2:22–23) teach us about the importance of prophets in the Bible?

4. What does this account teach us about God's judgment?

5. Where do we see God's grace and goodness in this text? In other words, does this account demonstrate anything about God's loving attitude toward the people of Israel?

6. Do you think the boys in the story were deserving of being mauled by bears? Why or why not.

7. Are there parts of Scripture you find unbelievable or unworthy of obedience? How should the story of the forty-two youths affect how you approach both the message and the messengers of Scripture?

8. How will God ultimately deal with our sin? How does Jesus repair the curse of sin and death under which we suffer?

2

Pillar of Salt — Genesis 19

As morning dawned, the angels urged Lot, saying, "Up! Take your wife and your two daughters who are here, lest you be swept away in the punishment of the city." But he lingered. So the men seized him and his wife and his two daughters by the hand, the Lord being merciful to him, and they brought him out and set him outside the city. And as they brought them out, one said, "Escape for your life. Do not look back or stop anywhere in the valley. Escape to the hills, lest you be swept away." And Lot said to them, "Oh, no, my lords. Behold, your servant has found favor in your sight, and you have shown me great kindness in saving my life. But I cannot escape to the hills, lest the disaster overtake me and I die. Behold, this city is near enough to flee to, and it is a little one. Let me escape there—is it not a little one?—and my life will be saved!" He said to him, "Behold, I grant you this favor also, that I will not overthrow the city of which you have spoken. Escape there quickly, for I can do nothing till you arrive there." Therefore the name of the city was called Zoar.

The sun had risen on the earth when Lot came to Zoar. Then the Lord rained on Sodom and Gomorrah sulfur and fire from the Lord out of heaven. And he overthrew those cities, and all the valley, and all the inhabitants of the cities, and what grew on the ground. But Lot's wife, behind him, looked back, and she became a pillar of salt.

—Genesis 19:15–26

ANCIENT MYTHOLOGIES AND FAIRYTALES tell stories of unfortunate people magically transformed into all sorts of non-human things. Greek mythology speaks of beautiful Medusa who, after having offended Athena, was turned into a snake-haired monster whose toxic gaze could subsequently turn her victims to stone statues. Similarly, Daphne, a beautiful nymph, cried out to the gods for help in an attempt to flee the advances of Apollo and was turned into a laurel tree for protection. I'm not sure the gods' "help" was very beneficial to Daphne. Of course, there are plenty of stories of princes and princesses being transformed into frogs and such. *Beauty and the Beast* recounts the tragedy of a handsome prince who, after telling an enchantress to get off his property, was cursed with ugliness. Such was the nature of this nefarious curse that only the love of a beautiful sassy book nerd named Belle could restore the beast to his former self.

Even the Bible contains a few stories of unpleasant metamorphoses. King Nebuchadnezzar was said to have been turned into something akin to an ass because of his asinine unwillingness to turn from his pitiful egoism and acknowledge God's supremacy over all creation (Dan 4:28–33). One night as he stood on the rooftop terrace of his palace, he gazed out over all that he had built (on the backs of slave laborers, of course) and marveled at his vast wealth (which he had stolen from neighboring kingdoms). Because of his arrogance, God cursed him so that his rational faculties left him. He was driven out into the wild where he lived for seven years. He ate grass like an ox, his hair grew out like the well-coiffed locks of an 80's glam rocker, and his nails turned into Freddy Krueger claws, or something to that effect, if my memory serves me correctly. The story is rather dramatic.

But perhaps the most intriguing biblical-curse-transformation-death story is found in Genesis, where we meet a woman known only as Lot's wife.[1] Apparently, she wasn't important enough to be named in the story. It's like in an action movie when you have a team of protagonists consisting of the main character, the important sidekick, and the cool other guy who is given a couple of funny lines here and there. But then you also have the three or four *other* other guys who hang out in the background. These are known in the credits as "Guy in the background #1," "Guy in the background #2," and you guessed it, "Guy in the background #3." They're insignificant to the overall story and only create compelling action scenes in which their death generates a sense of peril. Lot's wife was one of these

---

1. Lot's wife's namelessness in the text is possibly a slight to her for her lack of faith and righteousness.

unfortunate characters. In Genesis 19, "Woman in the background #1" was fleeing the destruction of Sodom, Gomorrah, and the other condemned cities of the plains, when she disobeyed God by looking back. As punishment, she was turned into a lovely salt statue and placed in the Louvre's Cour Puget sculpture garden, or something to that effect.

I think transmuting a person into salt is an original way to kill. King Midas turned his daughter into gold, accidently. But gold gets a bit boring. Here, however, a person is caught up in the cataclysm that befell the cities of the plains, and the result was a salt gargoyle. Salt, or sodium chloride (NaCl), is an essential nutrient for human health. Apparently, it contributes to nerve health. So, you could reason that Lot's wife now serves as an excellent seasoning in soups and salads, and an important mineral that contributes to a healthy and balanced diet. Bear in mind, however, that overconsumption of salt can lead to high blood pressure, heart disease, and stroke. My generalist brought that to my attention. But I digress. In any case, remember the salt vampire in *Star Trek: The Man Trap*, from the original series. That thing was ugly. After killing "Guy in red shirt #2," it was finally hunted down by Captain Kirk. The salt-sucking freak ended up on the wrong end of a Star Fleet issued type-two phaser set to kill. Don't mess with Captain Kirk.

A key feature of the story of "Woman in the background #1" is found in the phrase, "Lot's wife . . . looked back." We don't know what it was exactly that prompted her to pause, turn, and look back toward the plains. She was told to keep her eyes fixed forward and to run toward the salvation God had mercifully provided her. *No* hesitation, *no* pause, *no* lingering doubt.

HOLDING ON

The story of Lot's wife picks up after the infamous attempted rape incident in Sodom. Lot had settled among the people of the wicked cities of the plains after parting ways with his uncle Abraham (see Gen 13). One day, two angels in human form showed up in Sodom near evening. Their mission was to evaluate the unrighteousness of Sodom's inhabitants and carry out God's judgment against the city. Though Abraham had pleaded for mercy on behalf of Sodom for Lot's sake, God knew the extent of Sodom's evil, and he knew what would befall the city by his own hand. Lot invited the angels into his home for the evening, at which point the men of the city surrounded the house, like a mob of ravenous zombies to have their way with the visitors. Lot was about to toss his virgin daughters into the mob so his guests could make their escape out the back door, you know, like loving fathers do. But the angels made a completely awesome angel move and struck the men of Sodom with blindness.

At this point in the story, we see that hesitation and distrust are recurring themes. The angels told Lot to gather all who belonged to him and flee the city before it was overthrown by God's judgment. Those belonging to Lot would have included his wife, his daughters, and the men pledged to be married to his daughters. Hesitation and distrust first show up in the sons-in-laws-to-be who thought Lot was joking. They chose to stay behind. We see hesitation and distrust again in Lot, who continually stalled and asked that he be allowed to flee only to a nearby city, rather than to the mountains. God had sent a means of salvation, but Lot seems to have accepted it begrudgingly. This is evidenced by the fact that the angels seized him and his family and pulled them along. Lot's foolishness is mirrored by his wife, who in the fray, tarried and turned to look back in disbelief as her home was swept away.

The Lord rained down fire on Sodom, Gomorrah, and the surrounding villages. Here is where you may get a little hung up on the miracle of divine judgment. As I've noted elsewhere, and as with anything in Scripture that so much as hints at divine intervention, we may be tempted to interject a naturalistic explanation: It was an earthquake that awakened sulfur and burning gases from the reeking bowels of the earth; it was a meteorite that just happened to be in the wrong place at the wrong time; it was a meltdown at the local nuclear power plant.

Sure.

Some of those are reasonable possibilities. It's also possible that God sent down a fiery brimstone shower by his divine power. The point is not where the sulfur came from, but why it was sent, and by whom. As commentator Bruce Waltke rightly points out: "It is theologically mischievous to dismiss either the scientific causes of historical events because of theological explanation or vice versa."[2] In other words, anything is possible. God can use whatever means he chooses to exact judgment against those whose hearts are turned against him, and whose actions testify to their spiritual impoverishment. The irony, as Matthew Henry notes, is that "*hell* was rained down from *heaven* upon them."[3]

2. Waltke and Fredricks, *Genesis*, 279.
3. Henry, *Commentary on the Whole Bible*, 48. Emphasis mine.

Lot's wife, or what remained of her, was left to stand guard over a desolate place. The text says nothing of whether her corpse was simply coated with salty residue from the cataclysm, or whether she was transformed on a molecular level into a salt pillar. What is clear is that her salty carcass served as a visual reminder of her reluctance to flee for her life. In fact, to this day, salt-ridden formations can be found around the Dead Sea in Israel. The area is aptly named. The lake and surrounding area are largely devoid of life. Hypersaline water is toxic. In any case, salt—a substance that preserves—not only preserved the body of Lot's wife, it also immortalized her as an example of disobedience.

The punishment is both just and tragic. It was also a natural consequence of lingering behind, rather than moving urgently ahead. However, the central concern in this portion of Genesis 19 is that Lot's wife *looked back*. The Hebrew word *nebat*, meaning *to look*, has connotations of beholding, watching, or even considering with some pleasure or delight, as in Psalm 13:3. One might wonder if this was a simple backward glance over the shoulder. Perhaps it was curiosity that led her to sneak a peek at whatever exciting form of judgment God enacted on Sodom. After all, who hasn't slowed down to gawk at an accident on the side of the road. Was the sin of Lot's wife her careless voyeurism, or was it something more profound?

The explanation that a careless backward glance caused severe judgment doesn't fully capture the nature of the punishment. The text implies Lot's wife made an intentional effort to look. She seems to have paused to *consider* what she had been forced to leave behind. This understanding of the phrase "looked back" offers a more robust understanding of the situation and meshes well with the apostle Luke's reference to Lot's wife as an example of those who turn back from faithful obedience to the Christ they profess (Luke 17:31–2). The text is clear that Lot had also faltered in his obedience. He too had hesitated. But there was something different about his wife. This was more than hesitation.

It's not as if she suddenly realized she'd left the oven on and went back to double check. It wasn't a sudden awareness that she forgot to grab the old family photo albums and her grandmother's antique china. We shouldn't think that Lot's wife was solely trying to catch a final glimpse at her chic apartment with its rooftop pool and stunning views of the city skyline. I'm not even sure the fundamental problem was her sadness over the loss of her friends from her Saturday morning ladies book club. The problem was deeper. It was a problem of the heart. Her eyes weren't fixed on the savior who had graciously offered her a chance to escape the impending judgment. Her home and former life among a wicked people had permeated her soul, and she could not peel her heart away from the utter corruption she had left behind. She was looking back at what she thought would bring her ultimate comfort and security. She didn't fundamentally believe God had her best interests in mind as he led her up the mountain and out of the disaster below. Lot's wife seems to have cherished the values of Sodom and joined them in their demise. In essence, she had crafted an idol in her heart and that idol led to her ruin. She had looked back because her heart was leading her to go back.

LETTING GO

Reformer, John Calvin, famously said that "the human mind is, so to speak, a perpetual forge of idols."[4] Calvin aptly goes on to note that we substitute "vanity and an empty phantom in place of God."[5] We conceive idols in our minds that we then craft with our hands. We naturally make excuses to remain in places of comfortable idolatry and to coddle the idols we hold dear. I'll take this a step further. We hold on to our idols because we love our sin. We love to cling to the very things that slowly poison our souls and separate us from our creator. We continually look back, and even ponder with utmost attention, all that the world, the flesh, and the devil offer us. These are things we simply can't refuse. Sometimes we look back on our past and dwell in our shame, our fear, and our regret. Sometimes we sit in our hurt and dwell in our pain with no desire for forward movement toward forgiveness and restoration. The death of Lot's wife begs us to consider whether we are unwilling to let go. It begs us to ask why we choose to live in the comfortable places, even if those places are not good for our spiritual growth.

The lie of idolatry whispered from the dark recesses of our hearts is that if only I attain the unattainable god that lies just out of reach, I will be whole. I'll be complete once I've impressed my peer group and garnered their accolades. I'll be satisfied once I've sufficiently padded my retirement accounts. I'll be happy once I've crowned my education with a terminal degree from a prestigious university. I'll be whole once I've found full

4. Calvin, *Institutes*, 11:8, 55.
5. Ibid.

emotional support in my spouse. I'll be fulfilled once I've fed my addiction one last time.

False gods can't be attained because they are, by definition, unattainable. An *unreal* response will never satisfy a *real* need. "Woman in the background #1" represents every individual who makes up the countless multitude of those who look back. We've all been there. The place we've been called out from wants to call us back. We will want to turn. We will want to give ourselves to contemplative fixation on that ugly thing that lurks behind us. But the Lord takes his children by the hand and draws them away from that place (Ps 37:23–24).

As Lot and his family no doubt experienced, the journey to the mountains is wrought with peril. Easy flatlands and rolling hills are soon replaced by rock-laden paths up steep slopes. But God never promised ease. Instead, he promised salvation. Consider the words of Jesus to his disciples in Matthew 16:24–26:

> If anyone would come after me, let him deny himself and take up his cross and follow me. For whoever would save his life will lose it, but whoever loses his life for my sake will find it. For what will it profit a man if he gains the whole world and forfeits his soul? Or what shall a man give in return for his soul?

To deny ourselves is to deny the false gods we nurture in the deepest and most sacred corners of our heart. To follow Christ is to trust he has something better for us than what we've left behind. To take up our cross is to suffer in standing by our convictions even in the face of derision and apathy. To save our life is to entrust ourselves to the one who created us. God himself gives us the grace necessary to walk with him. He gives us a new identity. When the credits roll, we will not simply appear as "Miserable person in the background who looked back and died #1." As the apostle John relates, "to all who did receive him, who believed in his name, he gave the right to become children of God." In Christ, we are named. We are known. We are called "child of God."

STUDY QUESTIONS

1. How would you define idolatry? What are some idols of our culture?

2. Read the entirety of Genesis 19 and summarize what was about to befall the city of Sodom and its neighbors. In Genesis 19:15–26, what was Lot's overall reaction to the report of God's impending judgment of Sodom? How did the angels respond to Lot throughout these events?

3. Do you think Lot and his family trusted God through this process?

4. Think about the behavior of Lot's wife in Genesis 19:26. What do you think caused God to judge her? Was the judgment rooted in that she looked back, or was it rooted in something more?

5. It seems that Lot's wife was preoccupied with what she had left behind, rather than on the salvation that was laid out before her. Identify something that has preoccupied you and turned your own heart from God. What has caused you to "turn back"? What has caused you to stay focused on God?

6. What does the account of Lot's wife teach us overall about the character of God?

7. Read Matthew 16:24–26. Is it possible for our heart to be divided between God and other things? Explain. What does Jesus promise those who follow him?

8. Read John 8:31–32 and 2 Corinthians 3:17–18. Practically, how does faith in Jesus set us free from idolatry and sin? How can we find daily freedom in Jesus?

3

Shanked in the Gut — Judges 3

And the people of Israel again did what was evil in the sight of the Lord, and the Lord strengthened Eglon the king of Moab against Israel, because they had done what was evil in the sight of the Lord. He gathered to himself the Ammonites and the Amalekites, and went and defeated Israel. And they took possession of the city of palms. And the people of Israel served Eglon the king of Moab eighteen years.

Then the people of Israel cried out to the Lord, and the Lord raised up for them a deliverer, Ehud, the son of Gera, the Benjaminite, a left-handed man. The people of Israel sent tribute by him to Eglon the king of Moab. And Ehud made for himself a sword with two edges, a cubit in length, and he bound it on his right thigh under his clothes. And he presented the tribute to Eglon king of Moab. Now Eglon was a very fat man. And when Ehud had finished presenting the tribute, he sent away the people who carried the tribute. But he himself turned back at the idols near Gilgal and said, "I have a secret message for you, O king." And he commanded, "Silence." And all his attendants went out from his presence. And Ehud came to him as he was sitting alone in his cool roof chamber. And Ehud said, "I have a message from God for you." And he arose from his seat. And Ehud reached with his left hand, took the sword from his right thigh, and thrust it into his belly. And the hilt also went in after the blade, and the fat closed over the blade, for he did not pull the sword out of his belly; and the dung came out. Then Ehud went out into the porch and closed the doors of the roof chamber behind him and locked them.

When he had gone, the servants came, and when they saw that the doors of the roof chamber were locked, they thought, "Surely he is relieving himself in the closet of the cool chamber." And they waited till they were embarrassed. But when he still did not open the doors of the roof chamber, they took the key and opened them, and there lay their lord dead on the floor.

Ehud escaped while they delayed, and he passed beyond the idols and escaped to Seirah. When he arrived, he sounded the trumpet in the hill country of Ephraim. Then the people of Israel went down with him from the hill country, and he was their leader. And he said to them, "Follow after me, for the Lord has given your enemies the Moabites into your hand." So they went down after him and seized the fords of the Jordan against the Moabites and did not allow anyone to pass over. And they killed at that time about 10,000 of the Moabites, all strong, able-bodied men; not a man escaped. So Moab was subdued that day under the hand of Israel. And the land had rest for eighty years.

— JUDGES *3:12–30*

SOMETIMES SALVATION SHOWS UP in unexpected places. Saviors take unexpected forms. A poignant scene from J.R.R. Tolkien's *The Lord of the Rings* depicts four young hobbits (halflings) seeking refuge from their sinister pursuers—undead agents of evil called Ringwraiths. As the hobbits sit in a tavern waiting for Gandalf, their wise and powerful companion, to join them, they notice a strange and menacing man watching them from the corner of the room. Cloaked and hooded, the stranger observes them from a distance waiting for an opportunity. Unbeknownst to the hobbits, this stranger happens to be their salvation. More than a mere tavern scoundrel, the man is actually a powerful warrior and benevolent guide who would go on to deliver the hobbits from their pursuers and rescue Middle Earth from the malevolent sorcerer Sauron. In their moment of need, the mysterious stranger reveals himself to be Aragorn, king of men, protector of the innocent, ally to all good-hearted folk, and friend of hobbits. Aragorn is the unexpected salvation the hobbits need.

In a similar way, Judges 3:12–30 shows us that salvation comes in an unexpected form—Ehud, a calm, calculated, left-handed assassin who shanked Israel's corpulent oppressor in the gut with a glorified steak knife. Following the recurring theme of the Book of Judges, the story of Eglon and Ehud begins with Israel's sin. Because of this sin, God handed the nation over to Eglon, king of Moab, who oppressed the people for a time. When the oppressed nation inevitably called out to God for mercy, he answered them, remembering his people in their affliction. They were given a deliverer—a hit man who turned the tide with one thrust of his sword.

Attempts to over-spiritualize the passage fall short. The story of Eglon and Ehud is not written to teach us a lesson about the merits of good nutrition (don't get fat like Eglon). It is not written as a reminder that lefties are people, too (even though they're often accused of bad penmanship). The life and times of Eglon are not intended as a parable to dissuade us from naively trusting those who might turn out to be potential enemies, or to tell us something about how oppression doesn't pay off. This is simply a tale of blood and gore from the annals of Jewish history—a tale that never rears its ugly head in Sunday school curriculums or children's Bibles. For obvious reasons, we don't read this one to our kindergarteners. Even a toned-down cartoonish drawing of a crazy bloke stabbing a fat scalawag in the intestines would not sit well with most parents of preschoolers. Alas, the story of Eglon's death is found in the dark recesses of the Bible. But if we're to take the Bible seriously and learn from it, we need to read this account and deal with it.

The key to understanding this passage is found in verse 15. God raised up a deliverer. Israel cried out for help and God answered. God's people were in dire need, and he came to the rescue. Despite their sin, God loved the people with whom he had made his covenant. As commentator Dale Ralph Davis notes, "God didn't send a mere assassin, murderer, liar, or deceiver; he sent a savior."[1] His heart broke for his people as it always does and always will. The story of the death of Eglon is a story of salvation for those God chose to redeem according to his grace.

A MESSAGE OF RETRIBUTION

Eglon, king of Moab, and connoisseur of cookies, cakes, pies, and donuts, had enslaved God's beloved people—a people he had sworn by covenant to cherish, prosper, and save. This enslavement was part of God's design to get his wayward bride's attention, to draw her back to him. In other words,

1. Davis, *Judges*, 59.

Israel's rebellion didn't surprise God, nor infringe on his overall plan for his people. God withdrew his protection of Israel and "gave" the people over according to their own perverse desire as a gift to a wicked man. We see this theme often repeated in the Old Testament. Wicked people are used to judge the wickedness of other wicked people until those wicked people repent and their wicked oppressors are then judged in turn. Nothing escapes God's knowledge and providential oversight. God allowed his people's oppression to guide them to the painful recognition of their error. The goal was not pain itself, but restoration of his beloved people. His plan is always to draw out true devotion and obedience.

Sometimes the withholding of grace is judgment enough. The void of God's favor in Judges 3 left a very large gap, a gap that was filled, in this case, by a very large man. God's people had forsaken him, and so he left them to wallow in their rebellion by giving them what they deserved: Slavery to their sin and slavery to a foreign oppressor who would subjugate them and make their lives miserable. Considering the world's recent interest in body-positivity, it can seem uncouth to focus on Elgon's size. His size, however, is an important detail in the text. It is implicit in the passage that king Eglon was an oversized glutton of biblical proportions who made Fat Bastard of *Austin Powers* look like an emaciated 90s supermodel. He was so fat that when he stepped on a scale it said, "To be continued . . . ." He was so fat that when he wore a yellow robe, people yelled, "Taxi!" He was so fat his belt size was "equator." In fact, the latest cutting-edge archeological research (that I just made up) reveals Eglon enjoyed Chinese buffets and frequent visits to Krispy Kreme. He disliked CrossFit, crash diets, and long walks on the beach.

In the ancient world, his size was viewed as a sign of power and wealth. He could afford to lay around. He didn't need to work. Others did it for him.

This rotund ruler. This corpulent commander. This chunky chieftain was permitted, by God's sovereign design, to remind Israel of their forgotten dependence on him. God was, after all, the God who had rescued Israel out of Egypt, out of the land of slavery. God was the God who had given them his law and promised them salvation. God was the one who would send the Son, Jesus Christ, to be the savior of a world enslaved by sin.

This ultimate savior, Jesus Christ, is foreshadowed by lessor saviors throughout biblical history. One such savior was Ehud the Benjaminite, our left-handed man from Judges 3. Ehud was likely a typical lefty—smart, creative, talented, and attractive (like the author of this book, also a lefty).

However, in the ancient world, lefties were seen as deficient. The right hand was the dominant hand. To sit at someone's right hand was to be placed in a position of honor (Ps 16:11 and Isa 62:8–9). The left was relegated to the ignoble task of wiping residual excrement from one's rear end. It was the poop hand. It was the fecal matter appendage. Lefties were "special," in a bad way. Much like red-nosed reindeer, lefties didn't get picked first for the kickball squad, the mini-golf team, or spin the bottle.

Some scholars and commentators debate the meaning of Ehud's left-handedness. Bear in mind, Ehud is designated a Benjaminite, literally a "son of the right hand." The left-handed son of the right hand, single-handedly vanquished his foe in an underhanded way.[2] There's irony in the story. So, what of Ehud's left-handedness? The literal rendering of the text from the original Hebrew can suggest that Ehud was *unable* to use his right hand. Some purport that Ehud may have had a disability of some kind, making the use of his right hand impossible.[3] That reading seems to be a stretch, as the same Hebrew wording can also refer to a person having a dominant left hand. Ten percent of the total population is left-handed.[4] I would propose we take Ehud's left-handedness at face-value. He belonged to a ten percent minority.

I would also recommend the idea that God chose Ehud for a reason. Ehud's actions fit within God's providential plan for his people. Granted, it can seem odd that God would choose an assassin to deliver the very people he handed over to subjugation in the first place. Our own religious sensibilities whisper a gentle reminder that God isn't supposed to use assassins to kill people, no matter how bad they might be. But where do we get the notion that God is above assassination? Though violence is not God's moral will for his precious creation, the biblical narrative shows us a God who steps into the mess of human brokenness and sin, and acts upon, beside, and within human agents to accomplish his work of judgment and redemption.

God chose an unlikely hero. It seems it was Ehud's left-handedness that allowed him to slip past the guards. His right thigh (his sword thigh) was not checked since most warriors would have strapped their weapon to the left thigh. Maybe the pat down was incomplete. Maybe the guards were

2. Lilian R. Klein discusses the irony of Ehud's left-handedness in her commentary, *Triumph of Irony*, 37.

3. Keller, *Judges for You*, 47.

4. Jarry "Are You Left-Handed?"

just lazy. Either way, they let a dangerous man pass unhindered through the security screening. Moreover, Eglon foolishly dismissed his bodyguard so he could hear God's special message all for himself. His foolishness cost him his life. With his left hand, Ehud reached to the scabbard on his right thigh and drew his sword, plunging it into Eglon's swollen bulk.

We read that the sword was one cubit in length, the equivalent of about eighteen inches. One might imagine something akin to a small Greek style *xiphos* or an exaggerated prison shank. When Ehud thrust the sword into Eglon's gut, the passage denotes that the fat closed in around it. The entire sword disappeared into the lard, like Luke Skywalker's X-wing sinking into the mud on that swampy dump of a planet, Dagobah, where Yoda lived out his final days moving things around with his mind and plotting how to bring balance to the force. Perhaps Ehud's sword had no cross guard, explaining how the hilt sank into Eglon's flab.[5] It would also contribute to the concealability of the weapon.

I'd like to think Ehud hoisted the sword over his head, in true He-Man fashion, while crying out: "By the power of Grayskull!" But it seems he was a little more discreet than that. The irony of the passage is in Ehud's words to the king: "I have a secret message for you, oh king." I bear a message from God. Actions speak louder than words. A piece of tempered steal passed into Eglon's stomach, causing him to void his excrement as he passed into the agonizing arms of death. I pity whoever had to clean up that mess. No doubt, a feat of engineering would have been required to remove Eglon's body from his palace. The cleanup, however, wasn't Ehud's problem. While the guards waited outside the door, he escaped out the back way and ran to marshal an army that would go on to throw off Moabite subjugation in a bloodbath worthy of an over-the-top 80s action movie. Ehud's sword acted as the voice of God that fateful day.

A MESSAGE OF DELIVERANCE

A message from God is not something to take lightly. God gets the final word. God says exactly what he wants to say, whether by prophet, apostle, or in this case, assassin. Hebrews 4:12 reminds us that "the word of God is living and active, sharper than any two-edged sword, piercing to the division of soul and of spirit, of joints and of marrow, and discerning the thoughts and intentions of the heart." God's word cuts deeper than any

---

5. See Cundall, *Judges*, 76.

device forged by human hands. Hebrews 1:1 reminds us that in the past God spoke through prophets at various times and in various ways. God spoke the world into existence. There is power in his words. God can speak through burning bushes (Exod 3), through talking donkeys (Num 22), through writing on a wall (Dan 5), and in this particular case, through a sword to the abdomen. The story of King Eglon is a story of deliverance where God gets the final word.

Unfortunately, the deliverance afforded by Ehud's actions did not last. Israel was delivered. And what did they do with their new-found freedom? They got spiritually lazy, forgetting what God had done for them. They became complacent and turned their hearts to idolatry. Over and over Israel fell back into sin, back into enslavement, and back into desperation. Israel's incessant rejection of their Lord and Savior is testimony to the pathological nature of sin. To deny the fallen human condition and its effects is to deny reality itself. Philosophical viewpoints, such as Marxism and its critical theoretic progeny that deny the fallen nature of man, end up viewing human problems through the lens of power struggles rather than sin. The oppressed must throw off the oppressor, becoming oppressors themselves, necessitating further overthrow, *ad infinitum*. History proves that when the mechanisms of godless philosophies are employed for the purpose of restitution and justice, injustice ensues. Judges 3 tells us that oppression is what humans do when given the opportunity. Humans are jerks. Ehud didn't and couldn't end the oppression. He only provided a few years of respite (eighty to be precise). At best, Ehud's deliverance of the people only hints at the need for someone greater. At best, he is a reminder that oppression is a basic reality of human depravity, and deliverance is a basic need. At best, Ehud foreshadows a greater salvation.

God has spoken and he has a secret message for us today—an unlikely hero, born to an unlikely mother, in an unlikely fashion, in a lowly stable, in the small town of Bethlehem—that message is the Word made flesh, the Son of the living God, Jesus Christ (John 1:1). God's final revelation, his most wonderful and special message, is the incarnate Word. If you want to hear this secret message, send away the guard, close the doors, and lend him your ear: Jesus Christ has come to seek and save the lost, to set the captives free, to proclaim salvation to those living in sin and death. What Ehud only temporarily accomplished through his famous assassination attempt, Jesus did by giving his life once for all (Heb 10:10).

The message of Judges 3:12–30 is that God does not hesitate to speak into the ugliness of human sin. He uses ugly circumstances, ugly oppressors, and ugly actions to get our attention. He creates beauty out of ugliness. Furthermore, the God of the Bible does not hesitate to speak into our challenges and provide real solutions. When his people suffer, he hears them. When they sin, he disciplines them to draw them back to him in repentance. When they suffer, he comes alongside them and suffers with them, even unto death on a cross. God sends serious deliverers for serious problems. God gets the last word.

STUDY QUESTIONS

1. What characteristics would you generally look for in a savior?

2. Why were God's beloved people subjected to Eglon? What does this subjugation tell us about God's discipline of his children? See Hebrews 12:6.

3. In what ways do we see God's sovereign care for Israel in this story?

4. Does Ehud's left-handedness tell us anything about the kind of person he was and how others may have viewed him? Likewise, what does Eglon's corpulence tell us about his character?

5. How do we see God use Ehud? In what ways, if any, does Ehud act independent of God's direction?

6. Do you get the impression that Ehud's deceptive assassination is sanctioned by God? Explain. 7. Do you think Eglon got what he deserved? Explain why or why not.

7. In what way is Ehud's solution to Israel's oppression ultimately inadequate? Think of some things that "oppress" you, and from which you need deliverance (i.e. fear, guilt, shame, anxiety, relationships,

anger, addiction, or doubt, etc.). Do you think human beings can provide ultimate answers to our emotional, relational, and spiritual problems? Explain.

8. Ehud gave rest to the people for 80 years. In what ways does Jesus offer a greater salvation for his people than that of Ehud? See 1 John 4:14.

4

Defenestration, Pulverization, and Mastication — 2 Kings 9

And of Jezebel the Lord also said, 'The dogs shall eat Jezebel within the walls of Jezreel.' Anyone belonging to Ahab who dies in the city the dogs shall eat, and anyone of his who dies in the open country the birds of the heavens shall eat. (There was none who sold himself to do what was evil in the sight of the Lord like Ahab, whom Jezebel his wife incited).

—1 Kings 21:23–25

When Jehu came to Jezreel, Jezebel heard of it. And she painted her eyes and adorned her head and looked out of the window. And as Jehu entered the gate, she said, "Is it peace, you Zimri, murderer of your master?" And he lifted up his face to the window and said, "Who is on my side? Who?" Two or three eunuchs looked out at him. He said, "Throw her down." So they threw her down. And some of her blood spattered on the wall and on the horses, and they trampled on her. Then he went in and ate and drank. And he said, "See now to this cursed woman and bury her, for she is a king's daughter." But when they went to bury her, they found no more of her than the skull and the feet and the palms of her hands. When they came back and told him, he said, "This is the word of the Lord, which he spoke by his servant Elijah the Tishbite: 'In the territory of Jezreel the dogs shall eat the flesh of Jezebel, and the corpse of Jezebel shall be as dung on the face of the field in the territory of Jezreel, so that no one can say, This is Jezebel.'

—2 KINGS 9:30–37

THOUGH MOST OF US aren't willing to admit it, we want to be led. We want to be taken care of. We like good leaders. We like it when others make the hard decisions. We like it when they succeed to our benefit. And when they fail, we feel relief that at least we're not the ones who have to bear the inevitable public criticism that accompanies their lack of success. We like the idea of a good king. Even though modern democracy has its obvious benefits, the world's fascination with monarchy (and most specifically the British monarchy) signals its intrinsic desire to serve a worthy potentate. Some, including Aristotle, argue that the rule of a benevolent king is the best form of government.

Worthy potentates are hard to come by. The biblical books of 1 and 2 Kings are replete with stories of unworthy ones. Both the southern kingdom of Judah and the northern kingdom of Israel suffered under the godlessness of royal morons.[1] In both kingdoms, bad kings were succeeded by worse kings, with only a few exceptions. Then these worse kings were succeeded by worser kings. Finally, the very worst of kings finished the job of overseeing their nations' decline and utter failure. They accomplished this by morally and economically running their nations into the ground and eliciting exile at the hands of the Assyrians, who took the kingdom of Israel, and the Babylonians, who took Judah in the south.

Israel had a lot of bad kings . . . and bad queens. After all, I don't want to be sexist and leave out the amazing contributions women have made to human depravity. If you're going to be a total jackass, it's nice to have someone special by your side to play a supportive role. Every jackass needs a jillass, and vice versa. Clyde had Bonnie. Skeletor had Evil-Lyn. King Ahab had Queen Jezebel. Together, Ahab and Jezebel made a marvelous tabloid-worthy royal couple. I can't really comment on the condition of their marriage. All I know is that they had many common interests: Attending dinner

---

1. Because of Solomon's idolatry, God judged the national of Israel by dividing it into a southern kingdom of Juda, whose kings were descendants of David, and a northern kingdom consisting of 10 of Israel's tribes. See 1 Kings 11 and 12.

parties, playing pickleball, worshipping demonic gods, and murdering the Lord's prophets. The Israelite court under Jezebel's leadership was no doubt an exciting place. Intrigue, murder, Baal-worshipping debauches, and devilry of various creative kinds were, no-doubt, commonplace. Jezebel was a woman of violence who died a violent death.

The queen of Israel had a long resume of criminal activity. She was responsible for the mass execution of God's prophets (1 Kgs 18:4 and 13). She was a liar and conniver who had a law-abiding citizen falsely accused and murdered so she could seize his land for her husband (1 Kgs 21). She was also described as an instigator of "whorings" and "sorceries" (2 Kgs 9:22). The Hebrew word rendered "whore" (zenunim, in the 2 Kings text) can describe fornication or unfaithfulness. Such a description of Jezebel is fitting considering her affiliation with Baal worship and its cult of ritual sex. Baal was chief among the Canaanite deities and the bringer of rain and crop fertility—fertility being the key word here. The kinky part of Baal worship was the frequent sexual orgies that took place in Baal's temple.[2] Apparently, "going to church" meant something very different in ancient Canaan than it means today. While it's true that Jezebel's whorings and sorceries could refer more generally to her *unfaithfulness* to the God of Israel, it's more likely that since she was of Phoenician decent, the worship of YHWH would not have been a part of her life in the first place. We shouldn't necessarily rule out that whoring could refer to her regular attendance at, um, "church."

Jezebel and Ahab made for a great team. We read in 1 Kings 21:25: "There was none who sold himself to do what was evil in the sight of the Lord like Ahab, whom Jezebel his wife incited." Jezebel was no mere sidekick or mattress trull for Ahab; she was a consistent instigator of the royal couple's evil. She was the brains behind the operation, as proven by her cunning murder of Naboth (1 Kgs 21). I can see her now, lounging indolently on the throne, her lush body wrapped in a diaphanous gown, her red lips calling for the heads of the prophets, her cruel seductive eyes searching judiciously for signs of opposition to her dominion. There was no other quite like her—Jezebel the socialite, the celebrity, the personality, and glamourous original cast member of The Real Housewives of Canaan, ready to unleash hell on anyone who got in her way.

Yes, we long to follow good leaders, but Jezebel was not one of them. Even her apparent charisma could not salvage her career as queen of Israel. I guess if you're not going to be remembered as a good leader, you might

2. See Allbright, *Archaeology and the Religion of Israel.*

as well be remembered for living an exciting life and dying an exciting death. While most of us would be content to die in the least traumatic way possible, she went out with cringe-inducing style. In fact, Jezebel's death is noteworthy in that she died in three impressive ways: *Defenestration, pulverization,* and *mastication.* I'll explain below.

A BAD QUEEN'S DRAMATIC DEATH

The build up to Jezebel's demise is important in that her punishment fits her crimes. As Dale Davies notes, "the grossness of the judgement fits the wickedness of the offender."[3] Jezebel's feud with the prophet Elijah and all servants of the Most High God is legendary. The blood of God's prophets was on her hands, and Elijah, chief antagonists, was in her sights. Because of her crimes against the Lord, Elijah had prophesied:

> And of Jezebel the Lord also said, 'The dogs shall eat Jezebel within the walls of Jezreel.' Anyone belonging to Ahab who dies in the city the dogs shall eat, and anyone of his who dies in the open country the birds of the heavens shall eat (1 Kgs 21:23–24).

"Eaten by dogs" would certainly make for a great epithet on one's tombstone. But as exciting as that is, dogs only enter the picture after Jezebel had been thrown from a window and trampled by horses.

Defenestration—This delightful noun is rooted in the word *fenestration,* which refers to the arrangement of windows within a building. It's an architectural term. Bear in mind, however, that architecture can kill. People have been the unfortunate victims of staircases, loose masonry, poorly designed balconies, and in the case of Jezebel, open windows. To defenestrate someone is to throw them out of a window to their death. The term apparently originated with an incident in Prague where a couple of Ferdinand II's imperial governors were tossed from a castle window, sparking the Thirty Years War.[4]

In the account of Jezebel's death, Jehu, the newly anointed leader of the northern kingdom of Israel, had come to town to clean house. In keeping with the prophecies concerning the downfall of Arab and his progeny, Jehu showed up as an instrument of God's judgment. He also came to remove any remnants of a spent monarchy. As Jezebel observed the arrival of Jehu's

---

3. Davis, *2 Kings,* 157.
4. See Wedgwood, *Thirty Years War.*

entourage from the security of her palace, she must have known what was coming. She would die, and she would die with dignity, or so she thought. We read that she arranged her hair just right, checked her eye liner, applied some mascara, and went to the window to look out upon her executioner.

The exchange between the two is telling: "Do you come in peace . . . you murderer," seems a provocative statement on Jezebel's part. Jehu responded by looking to Jezebel's attendants and saying, "We can do this the hard way, in which case my men and I will fight our way up the stairs and kill everyone in our path, or we can do this the easy way in which case you can just throw the whore out the window and I'll spare your miserable lives." We read that "two or three eunuchs" were there. These eunuchs did the ballsy thing and threw Jezebel out the window. Her fall was likely not the graceful slow-motion leap at the end of *The Princess Bride*, where Buttercup gently glides into the arms of André the Giant. This was more akin to Judge Dredd throwing Mama, the drug boss, off the 200th floor of Peach Trees housing project in the 2012 movie *Dredd*, starring Karl Urban.

Pulverization—Once Jezebel's body contacted the ground below, she was promptly trampled by the horses of Jehu and his men (pulverized, to be precise). War horses make for great meat tenderizers. I've never been kicked by a horse, but as a young man working on my grandparents' dairy farm, I had many unpleasant encounters with cow hooves to the shin. Being beneath a hoof and the bulking creature to which it is attached is not conducive to any person's health.

One reason cavalry charges were effective in warfare was because not only would the opposing army be faced with your swords, spears, and shields, they would be faced with your swords, spears, and shields mounted atop a thousand-pound monster hurling toward them at thirty miles-per-hour. Death by trampling would not be pleasant, especially if the first hoof didn't promptly end your life. If Jezebel wasn't dead after being ridden over, I pity her. This brings us to the final piece of her brutal death, where the ravening dogs show up to contribute to the gore-fest.

Mastication—Let's pause to appreciate the complex process of teeth crushing and mixing food with digestive enzymes. As a child, I remember a teacher telling the class that for optimal digestion one must chew their food thirty times before shallowing. I have never done this. I doubt most people take their mastication of food this seriously. While the method of thorough chewing is an important first step in the digestive process, who is actually counting how many times they've chomped their food? Nobody.

Especially dogs. I have owned various dogs over the years. They will chew shoes, clothing, and furniture. I have rarely seen them chew food. Hungry dogs don't chew, they inhale.

Ironically, while Jehu was enjoying a well-earned lunch, the street dogs were enjoying a lunch of their own. After trampling Jezebel's body, Jehu was hungry. So, he entered the palace and helped himself to some matzo ball soup and a cheeseburger before realizing that it wasn't good form to leave Jezebel's body in the street. She was the former queen of Israel and daughter of the king of Sidon, a city on the Phoenician coast located in present day Lebanon. The princess of Sidon deserved a dignified burial at least. However, when Jehu's men went to attend to the body, there was no body left to attend to. The jackals had gotten there first, like when unattended steak is left within reach of a hungry pooch.

Second Kings 9 tells us the dogs saved the feet and hands as a snack for later. I'm not sure what they were planning to do with the skull, that also remained behind. Maybe they would drink mead from it like a bunch of Viking pillagers in celebration of a violent raid. Whatever the case, the few sundry body parts that remained were not worth collecting for burial. And so, the prophecy of Elijah was fulfilled. I can't think of a more dramatic death in Scripture than this one. It's a thing of horror. It's a thing of wonder. In a perverse way, it's a thing of beauty. You really can't make this stuff up. But why is it in Scripture, and why should we bother with such a disgusting story?

A GOOD KING'S ULTIMATE SACRIFICE

As previously noted, there are plenty of bad leaders in this world—narcissists, bullies, megalomaniacs, oppressors, and the like. Some of these leaders will continue in their roles unopposed. Others will be deposed. Queen Jezebel was a bad apple. You might say she got what she deserved—death. Jezebel, who stood arrogantly over the people, was thrown down. She who trampled God's prophets was trampled in turn. She who cultivated her beauty with great care was made ugly as dogs reduced her to a mere skull. She suffered greatly and died horribly as recompence for *her* evil. But as I ponder this, I can't help but think of another member of the Jewish royal family who also suffered greatly and died horribly as recompence for *our* evil. King Jesus gave sight to the blind and strength to the crippled. He preached mercy, justice, and forgiveness. He restored the broken and delivered those oppressed by the weight of their own sin. Though King of kings by divine birthright, and Lord of lords by divine nature, he was rejected by the very people he loved and faithfully served. King Jesus gave his life freely. He laid it down on behalf of his subjects, that they might enjoy enteral life by accepting him in faith. He laid down his life, only to take it up again in victory (John 10:18). He reigns now in justice, love, and grace. Jezebel died for *her* sins, Jesus died for *ours*.

Good kings and queens exhibit two important and seemingly opposing character qualities. On the one hand, they are people of humility, gentleness, and grace. On the other hand, their position of leadership necessitates justice, strength, and occasional brutality when dealing with lawlessness or foreign aggression. The former without the later makes for a pushover. The later without the former makes for a tyrant. As can be expected of Jesus, he exhibits the right formula by nature of his divine character.

Quoting from Zechariah 9:9, Matthew tells of the arrival of King Jesus in Jerusalem: "Say to the daughter of Zion, 'Behold, your king is coming to you, humble, and mounted on a donkey, on a colt, the foal of a beast of burden'" (Matt 21:5). The manner of Jesus' arrival in Jerusalem speaks to the gentleness and lowliness of his heart (Matt 11:29). In tenderness and love, he lowered himself from his position of honor and became a servant, submitting himself to the will of the Father (Phil 2:7–9). In this position of humility, he gave himself as a sacrifice for sin and allowed himself to suffer death, even death on a cross. Jesus is a loving king—an approachable king. He lets you get close, and he invites you to stay close each and every day as you follow him and learn the ways of the master.

The biblical God is not a god of imbalanced emotions or lopsided character traits. The full-orbed Jesus is one of love and wrath, compassion and justice, grace and judgment. What more can be expected of a truly good king? The wrath of God was seen in his judgment of our sin borne by Jesus at the cross. The wrath of God is also seen against those who mock his free gift of grace given by Jesus at the cross. The self-sacrifice of Jesus at the cross is an expression of the character perfections of God in his dealings with human beings. Scripture balances the smiling hippie Jesus of Christian bookstore kitsch with a muscled G.I. Joe action figure. Consider the description of Jesus in Revelation 19:11–16:

> Then I saw heaven opened, and behold, a white horse! The one sitting on it is called Faithful and True, and in righteousness he judges and makes war. His eyes are like a flame of fire, and on his

head are many diadems, and he has a name written that no one knows but himself. He is clothed in a robe dipped in blood, and the name by which he is called is The Word of God. And the armies of heaven, arrayed in fine linen, white and pure, were following him on white horses. From his mouth comes a sharp sword with which to strike down the nations, and he will rule them with a rod of iron. He will tread the winepress of the fury of the wrath of God the Almighty. On his robe and on his thigh he has a name written, King of kings and Lord of lords.

The Jesus of Revelation 19 doesn't play games. He cuts down devils with a Conan-the-Barbarian-style broadsword and pile-drives the wicked headfirst through the fabric of the universe. Good kings love their people with generosity and compassion. Good kings also crush their enemies while protecting the dignity of their reign and the welfare of their people.

Even the best of Israel's kings were inadequate to the task. King David was a man after God's own heart and the hope of Israel (1 Sam 13:14 and Acts 13:22). David was also a murderer, adulterer, and liar. He died surrounded by strife. King Hezekiah followed God with a pure heart and love for the law of the Lord. Hezekiah also foolishly allowed an envoy from Babylon to case the city of Jerusalem for future invasion (2 Kgs 20). His legacy was a waning kingdom a few generations away from overthrow. King Josiah led the people in righteousness and truth, turning the people back to the Lord and removing all hints of idolatrous worship from the land. Josiah was unable, however, to turn away God's wrath from a people that had been long steeped in rebellion. He died leaving his throne to his wicked son Jehoahaz (2 Kgs 23:31).

Jesus did what no other leader has been able to do. He lived a fully righteous life, taught God's word with authority and truth, brought eternal hope to Israel and left a legacy of generational disciples empowered by his Holy Spirit to fulfill his mission of redemption until he returns to consummate the final glorification of all creation. The contrast between Jesus and Jezebel is striking. In a world deficient of competent leaders, there is only one who will always get it right—Jesus Christ, the King of kings.

STUDY QUESTIONS

1. What would a ruler need to achieve during their reign for you to consider them successful?

2. What kind of leader was Jezebel? For context read 1 Kings 16:29–33, 18:1–15, and 21:25–26. Do you think you would have thrived or suffered under her reign?

3. In 2 Kings 9, as Jezebel prepares to meet her fate, what do you suppose is the purpose of Jezebel painting her eyes and adorning her head?

4. Describe the exchange that took place between Jehu and Jezebel? Do you think Jezebel would have survived had she been more diplomatic?

5. In what three ways did Jezebel die? Is there any significance to these manners of death? Does Jezebel's manner of death tell us anything about the kind of person she was?

6. What does the fulfillment of Elijah's prophecy teach us about God?

7. Read Ephesians 1:15–23. Consider the reign of Jesus from the right hand of the Father. In what ways does the reign of Jesus differ from the reign of all others?

8. Should a good leader exhibit love and grace, judgment and wrath, or both? Explain.

9. What does it mean for Jesus to be lord and king of your life? In what areas have you denied him lordship of your life?

5

Strange Fire — Leviticus 10

Now Nadab and Abihu, the sons of Aaron, each took his censer and put fire in it and laid incense on it and offered unauthorized fire before the Lord, which he had not commanded them. And fire came out from before the Lord and consumed them, and they died before the Lord. Then Moses said to Aaron, "This is what the Lord has said: 'Among those who are near me I will be sanctified, and before all the people I will be glorified.'" And Aaron held his peace.

—*Leviticus 10:1–3*

THE ACT OF WORSHIPPING God can be hazardous to one's health. I've unwittingly attended Christian worship services where I needed ear plugs and was in danger of being trampled in a mosh pit, seared by pyrotechnics, and asphyxiated by excessive smoke-machine usage. Perhaps worship music style is just a matter of taste, but I worry that the goal of some worship experiences is to wrongly create an emotional response that can only be satisfied by an even bigger and bolder emotional response, *ad infinitum*. This can only leave the worshipper unsatisfied and looking for the next fix. If worship isn't pointing you to God, you're likely only being fed a fleeting emotion. My preference, if I'm going to pull a muscle or be trampled, is to do so while participating in something athletic, not while worshipping. And if I'm going to lose my hearing, I'd rather do it at a proper heavy metal concert where a scorching guitar solo is being shredded on a custom ESP guitar through a Marshall stack. Let's do things right.

In some religions, both past and present, worship has incorporated singing, praying, dancing, acrobatics, self-flagellation, self-deprivation, firewalking, animal and human sacrifice, and ritual sex, along with a host of other things. These practices can come with obvious consequences: sprained ankles, broken limbs, burns, and gonorrhea. Human sacrifice can result in . . . surprise, surprise . . . human death. Meditating, while subsisting on a single grain of rice per day, can lead to starvation, physical agony, and bizarre spiritual epiphanies. Worship is clearly not for the faint of heart.

While extreme acts of worship can be dangerous, the gods themselves can also be dangerous. The most dangerous kinds of gods are *evil gods*, *feeble gods*, and *holy gods*.

Evil gods are dangerous because they often require evil of their worshippers, like the Canaanite deity Molech. Sacrifice to Molech is mentioned in numerous places in the Old Testament. It was strictly prohibited in Levitical law because it involved child sacrifice, often of the first-born son (Lev 20:2–5). Both king Ahaz and king Manasseh of Israel were said to have committed this abomination (2 Kgs 16:3; 21:6).[1] Pre-Christian pagan societies also practiced human sacrifice at various times in history. Mesoamerican peoples, like the Mayans, offered up human sacrifices as nourishment for the gods until the Spanish conquistadors arrived and decimated the local population by sneezing on them. The Norse god Odin was also known to have an appetite for human blood. His bloodlust ended when *Marvel Comics* cleaned up his image. Up until a few centuries ago, the worship of Kali in some Hindu sects was accompanied by human sacrifice.[2] Think: *Indiana Jones and the Temple of Doom*. The reality of human sacrifice shouldn't come as a surprise. Our modern religion of radical self-worship and individualism has led some civilized twenty-first century westerners to celebrate the sacrifice of aborted unborn children as an offering in honor of the god of sexual liberation and self-empowerment. Human sacrifice is alive and well. So, be careful what you venerate.

Next to the dangers of evil gods are those of *feeble gods*. Weak impotent gods are dangerous because they demand worship while providing no value to the worshipper and no glory to themselves. While technically any god other than the true and living God is powerless, I'm thinking of

---

1. For more on the cult of Molech see Day, *Molech*.
2. See Knipe, *Hinduism*.

the gods aptly mocked by the prophet Isaiah (Isa 44:9–20). The prophet points out the irony and stupidity of a man who goes out into the woods to cut down a tree with the threefold purpose of burning some of the wood for warmth, cooking his food over the wood coals, and carving an idol of the remaining wood. The same substance that's ignited and consumed in minutes is also the substance that is supposed to answer your ultimate questions and satisfy your deepest longings. Isaiah's point is simple: If this is the way you approach spirituality, you're an idiot.

Do you have questions about the origins of the universe? Look to the firewood. Do you want insight into the meaning of life? Look to the firewood. Is your marriage in shambles? Is your boss a jerk? Do you wish there was more to your miserable existence than the daily grind? Look to the firewood. The firewood created you. It loves you. It wants the best for you. Are you beginning to appreciate the absurdity?

Plenty have fallen victim to evil and powerless gods. But these kinds of petty gods are of little interest. The dangerous god we mustn't ignore is the one and only holy God of the universe—a God so great, so powerful, so majestic, and so worthy of praise that to approach him cloaked in sin and irreverence is to invite judgment. Nadab and Abihu learned this valuable lesson the hard way.

HOLINESS IS A DANGEROUS THING

Aaron and his sons were the ancient Israelite equivalent to a modern church worship band. They were supposed to lead the people in the worship of God. Unfortunately, they did a shabby job. The sons of Aaron offered "unauthorized fire" before the Lord. We don't know what the unauthorized fire was exactly. What we do know is that the Lord had instructed his *holy* people how to practice *holy* worship of a *holy* God. Holiness is the key word. It means set apart or separate from other things. God is set apart. He is not on the same plane or level as anything else.

R.C. Sproul points out that holiness is not merely an attribute of God, but that it qualifies all other attributes.[3] God's love is holy. His grace is holy. His justice is holy. His character traits and essential nature exist on a greater level than anything we can exhibit through our meager imitations of these traits. In fact, Sproul rightly points out that holiness is the only quality of

---

3. Sproul, *Holiness of God*, 57.

God raised to the third degree.[4] "Holy, holy, holy is the Lord God almighty" (Isa 6:3; Rev 4:8). One practical implication of God's holiness is this: Our practices of worship must not resemble the worship of idols. They must not integrate heathen ritual. The worship of God must be set apart. No doubt, the unauthorized fire offered by Nadab and Abihu was unholy. This offering stood outside the prescribed and acceptable sacrifices God had established to prepare his people for the coming of Jesus—the ultimate and final sacrifice for sins. Their sacrifice was an offense to the holiness of the God who had created, delivered, and instructed his people.

But isn't worship supposed to be a free, uninhibited expression of our feelings? Didn't king David strip down and shake it on the dance floor as an act of worship (2 Sam 6:14–15)? Isn't worship supposed to be whatever we want to make it as long as we're sincere? Doesn't God love our silliness, our messiness, and our creativity? Well, kind of. Maybe. A few qualifications are needed, of course. I would suggest caution when taking creative liberties with worship. As an obviously stupid example, throwing human excrement at each other while running around the church sanctuary in devil costumes is certainly silly, messy, and creative. Does it honor the Lord? I can't see how it would. Rather, it's in our best interest to take our cues on the worship of God from God himself. This is why most Christian worship practices include things prescribed in Scripture, like prayer (Eph 6:18), preaching (2 Tim 4:2), communion (1 Cor 11:23–26), and the singing of hymns and songs of praise (Eph 5:19).

Blatant sacrilege is one thing, ignorance or carelessness is another. It's easy to see why God would punish blasphemy; it's hard to imagine that God would punish carelessness. And carelessness seems to be the only sin Aaron's sons committed, if any. What was their crime after all? They threw a little extra incense on the fire. That seems trivial, as if they had improvised and sung the bridge of their favorite worship chorus twice instead of once, or as if their sermon went too long when the congregation just wanted to get on with the potluck. The punishment seems unfair, but it's only unfair if we lack an appreciation for God's holiness.

Granted, there are plenty of fanciful naturalistic explanations for why Nadab and Abihu perished in the fire. Maybe they got carried away and built the fire too big. In their excitement to burn incense, they fell into the fire and died. Maybe they were throwing a kegger with their frat buddies and Nadab bet Abihu he couldn't jump over the fire. Abihu took the bet,

4. Ibid., 40.

46

and when his tunic caught fire, he forgot to stop, drop, and roll. His brother tried to help, and before you know it, they were both incinerated.

Actually, I know what it was. Nadab was wearing too much hair spray. Fire and hair spray are not a good combo. Or maybe they found a can of gasoline that their dad Aaron left in the garage and thought they'd have some fun. Whatever it was, it couldn't have been divine fire. Certainly God doesn't inflict the church worship team with spontaneous combustion, does he?

A holy God will be honored by his people. If God's holiness is akin to a glass of pure water, then our unholiness is a glass of water with varying degrees of poison and filth added in. Naturally, he would not let our pollution mingle with his purity. No unholy thing can look upon the face of God and live (Exo 33:20). The story of Isaiah's encounter with God in Isaiah 6 is evidence of this. Isaiah woke up in the throne room of the Most High God and was overcome by the glory of God and the majesty of his angels, called seraphim. Terror ensued.

It is important that we rid our minds of cartoonish notions of God and his angelic servants. Angels are probably not fat naked babies with cute little bows and arrows, nor are they attractive Swedish models in white gowns. The appearance of angels in Scripture is usually described as disorienting and horrifying (see Ezek 1, for example). Likewise, God is not a well-proportioned old man with a white beard who floats about on a cloud, in spite of what Michelangelo and his Sistine Chapel ceiling suggest. God is spirit (John 4:24); he is light (1 John 1:5); he dwells in unapproachable light (1 Tim 6:16). Notice that Isaiah doesn't even attempt a description of the Lord; he only *speaks* of *unspeakable* glory and the train of a robe flowing from a throne. The presence of a robe could be meant to represent the authority and majesty of the glory that overwhelmed the prophet. It was a kingly garment. Isaiah found out that entering the throne room of God is no joke. He looked toward the throne and before he could utter whatever expletive he was about to utter in slack-jawed shock, he knew that he was in danger of death. "Woe is me! For I am lost; for I am a man of unclean lips, and I dwell in the midst of a people of unclean lips; for my eyes have seen the King, the Lord of hosts!" (Isa 6:5). The impure had entered the presence of the pure. The unholy was standing before the holy. The creation had encountered the creator. Only an act of grace allowed Isaiah to survive the encounter.

If you want to appreciate the dangers associated with your miserable sinful self, entering the presence of the thrice holy God, read Leviticus 16. The whole chapter walks us through the extensive Day of Atonement sacrifices and ritual purification the high priest had to undergo before he was even allowed behind the curtain into the holy of holies—the innermost sanctuary where God's presence would descend into the cloud of smoke emanating from the lamp stands. The ceremony was precise. The cleansing rituals were meticulous. The donning of sacred garments was critical. The blood of the sacrificed animal must be sprinkled exactly seven times on the mercy seat of the arch of the covenant. Sufficient smoke from the burnt incense must veil the eyes of the priest so he wouldn't inadvertently gaze on the glory of God in its fullness and be struck down. Some traditions claim that a rope was tied around the high priest's ankle so that in case he was struck by God during the ritual, his charred carcass could be dragged back to the safe side of the curtain where his fellow priests awaited.

So, who wants to lead worship?

WORSHIP AT YOUR OWN RISK

The holiness of God did not go away after Jesus bore the wrath of God at the Cross. Jesus didn't come to live among us in love simply to help God outgrow his holiness. We sometimes think that the holiness of God is a disease from which the almighty had to recover. But God hasn't changed, even if our status before him has. God is an all-consuming fire (Deut 4:24; Heb 12:29). "It is a fearful thing to fall into the hands of the living God" (Heb 10:31). Worship of the thrice holy God is no joke. Nadab and Abihu learned this the hard way and were roasted in the oven of God's righteousness and then served as a warning with a side of mashed potatoes and a dinner salad. God's judgment comes in regular and extra crispy, and we earn it when we fail to honor the God who is perfectly within his divine rights to destroy us in our rebellion and sin.

Sometimes the God of grace and justice judges as an example to his people. Other times, he stays his hand as a demonstration of his compassion. This leniency doesn't mean he passively allows our mockery of his majesty and the trivialization of worship. It means he acts in wisdom for his glory and for the overall edification of those who would submit to his will and enjoy his goodness.

The story of the judgment of Nadab and Abihu was a rare act of God and an important pedagogical moment. Once was enough to teach generations of worshippers of the seriousness of the trivialization of worship when the object of that worship is the holy God of the universe. Modern worshippers might learn something from the life and death of Aaron's sons.

Christians risk trivializing worship when we go through the motions with no real intellectual or emotional investment. When we enter the presence of God on Sunday mornings (or whenever we happen to attend worship services), we best arrive prepared. Preparation means making ready our hearts and minds. It would certainly benefit us to prayerfully seek the Lord and quiet our hearts as we anticipate our time of corporate singing, reading, praying, and partaking in the Lord's Supper. Sunday morning worship is neither a talent show, a stand-up routine, a concert, nor anything other than an opportunity to enter the presence of God and acknowledge his divine perfections while being instructed in his ways and drawn to him in faith.

The trivialization of worship also happens when we reduce our concept of worship to a few trite and self-centered pop songs sung on Sunday morning. The object of worship (God) is infinitely more worthy of worship than the subject who does the worshipping (us). If worship makes us feel good, that's fine. It should, because worship is what we were created to do. But if our sole purpose in attending or leading worship services is to get a spiritual high, we've missed the point. The content of worship should be God-centered. Our songs should say something about who God is and what God has done. They should instruct us in the reality of creation, human fallenness into sin, salvation by the cross of Christ, and the restoration of creation that will take place at the glorious return of our Lord.

Worship that eradicates the sacred elements of ritual and that effaces the distinctly biblical vocabulary of the Christian faith for the sake of appearing innocuous to the unchurched will effectively harm the church. Theologically anemic worship lacks the nutritive qualities of biblically robust adoration of the one and only true God. The whims of popular culture cannot sustain Christian worship. Followers of Jesus can do better. The world needs better.

Go to Jesus with confidence in what he has done for you. But also go to Jesus with reverence and humility. Jesus might be our buddy. After all, he was a friend of sinners. But remember that he's also our Lord and King. The apostle John saw this clearly. The same John who had a privileged friendship with Jesus and reclined against him at the last supper (John 13:23) fell down in terror before the resurrected and glorified Christ (Rev 1:16–18). When John saw the vision of heaven, he didn't glibly and pretentiously high-five Jesus, while uttering, "Hey bro, how you been?" He dropped to the ground, as though dead, at the shear sight of the overwhelming glory of King Jesus who judges the quick and the dead and who slam dunks devils into the lake of fire.

The Bible leaves room for humans to *be* human in worship. We are invited to bring our offerings, talents, gifts, burdens, past, and pain. But in all of this, let's remember who it is we worship. Because of the shed blood of Jesus Christ at the cross, believers in Jesus can boldly approach the throne of grace with confidence (Heb 4:16). Confidence, however, does not mean arrogance. Nor does it mean foolishness. It does not mean triteness, silliness, or conceit. Believers are "in Christ." This means that the Father views us through that lens. It means believers view God through that lens. Being in Christ does not make his holiness go away. Rather, the indwelling of the Spirit of Christ in the believer augments understanding of the holiness of God. It gives believers a fuller and more beautiful picture of the holiness of God—a holiness expressed in love and justice. To worship is to celebrate the holiness of God with gladness in our hearts. The right way to approach the Lord in worship is with profound appreciation for the sacrifice that Jesus, the ultimate sacrificial lamb and high priest, accomplished on our behalf.

STUDY QUESTIONS

1. How would you define the act of worship? Is worship more than music? If so, what other elements belong in a worship service?

2. Which aspects of worship are most appealing to you in the contemporary church? Which might be off-putting?

3. Read Leviticus 10:1–3. Who were Nadab and Abihu and what seems to have been their offense?

4. A primary reason for offerings and sacrifices in the Old Testament was to point the people to the need for a greater and final offering in the blood of Jesus Christ. So, why would God care so much about the kinds of offerings presented to him?

5. Read Isaiah 6:1–7. What does Isaiah's encounter with God teach us about the kind of God we worship?

6. Read Hebrews 12:28–9. Is there a right and wrong way to approach God in worship?

7. Do you think God was just in his punishment of Nadab and Abihu? Explain your answer.

8. Who is Jesus Christ and what has he done that should incite our worship?

6

Witches, Ghosts, and Bloody Death — I Samuel 28

When Saul saw the army of the Philistines, he was afraid, and his heart trembled greatly. And when Saul inquired of the Lord, the Lord did not answer him, either by dreams, or by Urim, or by prophets. Then Saul said to his servants, "Seek out for me a woman who is a medium, that I may go to her and inquire of her." And his servants said to him, "Behold, there is a medium at En-dor."

So Saul disguised himself and put on other garments and went, he and two men with him. And they came to the woman by night. And he said, "Divine for me by a spirit and bring up for me whomever I shall name to you." The woman said to him, "Surely you know what Saul has done, how he has cut off the mediums and the necromancers from the land. Why then are you laying a trap for my life to bring about my death?" But Saul swore to her by the Lord, "As the Lord lives, no punishment shall come upon you for this thing." Then the woman said, "Whom shall I bring up for you?" He said, "Bring up Samuel for me." When the woman saw Samuel, she cried out with a loud voice. And the woman said to Saul, "Why have you deceived me? You are Saul." The king said to her, "Do not be afraid. What do you see?" And the woman said to Saul, "I see a god coming up out of the earth." He said to her, "What is his appearance?" And she said, "An old man is coming up, and he is wrapped in a robe." And Saul knew that it was Samuel, and he bowed with his face to the ground and paid homage.

Then Samuel said to Saul, "Why have you disturbed me by bringing me up?" Saul answered, "I am in great distress, for the Philistines are warring against me, and God has turned away from me and answers me no more, either by prophets or by dreams. Therefore, I have summoned you to tell me what I shall do." And Samuel said, "Why then do you ask me, since the Lord has turned from you and become your enemy? The Lord has done to you as he spoke by me, for the Lord has torn the kingdom out of your hand and given it to your neighbor, David. Because you did not obey the voice of the Lord and did not carry out his fierce wrath against Amalek, therefore the Lord has done this thing to you this day. Moreover, the Lord will give Israel also with you into the hand of the Philistines, and tomorrow you and your sons shall be with me. The Lord will give the army of Israel also into the hand of the Philistines."

—*1 Samuel 28:5–19*

The battle pressed hard against Saul, and the archers found him, and he was badly wounded by the archers. Then Saul said to his armor-bearer, "Draw your sword, and thrust me through with it, lest these uncircumcised come and thrust me through, and mistreat me." But his armor-bearer would not, for he feared greatly. Therefore Saul took his own sword and fell upon it. And when his armor-bearer saw that Saul was dead, he also fell upon his sword and died with him. Thus Saul died, and his three sons, and his armor-bearer, and all his men, on the same day together.

—*1 Samuel 31:3–6*

WITCHES SHOW UP FREQUENTLY in history and in fiction. Real witches are often less interesting than the fictional variety—you know, the hideous old hags with warts protruding from their unnaturally long hooknoses. Their unkempt black hair and black robes cover their even blacker hearts. Hunchbacked and wrinkled, they ride through the night on broom sticks casting spells on the unsuspecting and making general mischief. Witches were thought to be behind many a medieval misfortune. They were poisoners of wells and souls. They were responsible for impotence and crop failure. Witches were conjurers of spells and kidnappers of children. They crept through night shadows summoning devils and cursing God. Hedge witches. Bog witches. Kitchen witches. And most nefarious of all were the brew witches who were responsible for contaminating beer and spoiling everyone's fun.[1]

A cursory glimpse into history reveals we have had a longstanding obsession with and fear of witches, warlocks, sorcerers, magicians, enchanters, necromancers, wizards, and occultists of various kinds. The esoteric arts have confused, enticed, and revolted generations. Modern witches—practitioners of wicca and other forms of neo-paganism—are trying to change the negative image. They have largely succeeded. Witchy book sales are on the rise.[2] Witchy crystals are readily available. Witchy witches can be found in every major town across America. Witches may still baffle us. But more and more, people are getting used to the idea.

Real life witches, who are generally benevolent and oriented toward environmental concerns, are now more commonly accepted by society.[3] As the influence of the contemporary Christian church wanes, more people are turning to alternative spiritual practices. Interest in esoteric arts is growing. By venerating pantheistic natural forces, practitioners of witchery are not confined to the box of traditional theism. The "old ways" are alive. Witches are no longer viewed as demonic old crones, but are now reimaged as fun-loving environmentally sensitive caretakers of all living things. They are even sexy, believe it or not. *Bewitched* brought us Samantha. She was a classy lady who used her powers to make everyone's life a little better. Likewise, *Sabrina the Teenage Witch* made witchery cute. We certainly can't exclude Harry Potter and his consort of witchy friends from the discussion. Some might wonder whether we got the whole witch thing wrong. If you really think about it, Snow White was portrayed as a naïve bimbo. On the contrary, her wicked stepmother (aka wicked queen-*witch*) was a mature, confident, and attractive woman who knew what she wanted in life.

Historically, Christians and witches have not gotten along well. There are good reasons for this. The contrast in fundamental worldview assumptions is striking. Christians look heavenward to an all-powerful, creator God. Witches, generally speaking, look downward to the earth and the power contained within it and all living things. Christians view the human

---

1. Yes, brew witches were apparently a problem at various times in history. See Perozzi and Beaune, *Naked Pint*, 41–2.

2. Grossman, "Witch Books Hold Power."

3. Rabinovitch and Lewis, *Encyclopedia of Modern Witchcraft*.

condition as a problem of sin and separation from God. Witches view the human condition as a lack of honor for the elements of nature and failure to allow these elements to affect the cycles and energies within our own bodies. Christians claim there is one way to God: Faith in Jesus Christ. Witches claim to respect the diversity of practices that lead each unique individual on their own faith path. Christians root their faith in the historical realities of the life, death, and resurrection of Jesus. Witches' beliefs are an esoteric nebula defined and practiced by the individual. For Christians, the solution to life's ultimate questions and longings is found outside of one's self, in the person of Jesus Christ. For practitioners of witchcraft, one must look within. Christianity and witchcraft are incompatible belief systems. They follow vastly different means to achieve vastly conflicting ends.

In 1 Samuel 28, we read that witches—mediums and necromancers—had been put out of the land of Canaan by Saul, the first king of Israel. God's law forbade occultic practices (Lev 19:31 and Exod 22:18). Witchcraft was forbidden because it stood in direct opposition to the power of God. Witchcraft called its adherents to trust in something other than the God who had delivered the people of Israel out of the land of slavery in Egypt. Witchcraft demanded worship of a lessor power than he who had created the heavens and earth. It's ironic that the very practices Saul had undone would be his undoing. Witches were hard to come by in Saul's day, but he managed to find one in a place called En-dor.

LOOKING FOR ANSWERS IN THE WRONG PLACES

By the time we arrive at 1 Samuel 28, Saul had rejected God. Likewise, God had rejected Saul. But Saul needed answers. The Philistine army had come to wage war. What would be the outcome of the battle? He inquired of the Lord, but got nothing. No visions. No dreams. No prophetic words. No response from the *Urim*—objects attached to the breastplate of the high priest and used in lot-casting to determine the will of God. So, what do we do when we pray and get no immediate answer? In our good moments we might wait patiently for God to answer us according to his will and in his perfect timing. That would be the right way to do things. In our bad moments we might get impatient and take matters into our own hands. Sadly, some Christians finish their prayers and immediately turn to the tarot cards, astrological readings, and other dubious backup plans. That's what Saul thought, too. Our lack of trust in God is sometimes manifested in outrageous human solutions. Saul's most serious problem was not that he died a violent death in battle, though that was a problem. His real issue was a lack of trust in God and submission to God's will. Saul sought answers in places he never should have been looking.

We read that Saul had put the mediums and necromancers out of the land of Israel. It seems odd then that he would seek the services of such. I imagine the conversation with his men to have gone something like this:

"Find me a witch!" bellowed the king petulantly.

"But you drove them all out of the land," responded Saul's confused servants as they looked uncomfortably at one another.

"Then find me a sorceress," retorted the king, annoyed at the dimwittedness of his men.

"But sire, isn't that the same thing?"

"Enough fools! A medium or necromancer will do!"

At this, the men finally gave up. "As you wish your Highness. Why didn't you just say so in the first place."

Immediately, his servants directed him to a medium who lived in a place called En-dor. Why she was allowed to remain in the land, and how Saul's men knew of her is unspecified in the text. The exact location of En-dor has been the subject of debate. Saul's visit to the witch may have put him behind Philistine lines. Whatever the case, Saul was in desperate need, and so he hastened to seek her counsel.

We don't know much about the witch of En-dor. A little speculation might be in order. First, we must establish whether she was of the sexy-Halloween-costume-party-witch variety, or whether she was a hideous old crone? No one knows. But I think the mood of the story calls for a grizzled old fossil. We'll call her Gertrude. Second, we must set the stage for this creepy encounter. Though there's no scriptural or archeological evidence to support my theory, I would suggest the witch of En-dor lived in a candy house on the outskirts of Israel. She spent her time grooming her black cat, baking children in her state-of-the-art restaurant-quality oven, and stirring green frothing liquids in a cauldron while an eerie fog blew through the dead trees that lined the graveyard at the edge of her property. The moon was full. The night was black. But Saul wasn't afraid. When his men double-dared him to march up to the door, he did so with no reservation. He was a man on a mission.

On a more serious note, their exchange is interesting. The witch did not immediately recognize the king, but played her cards cautiously, nonetheless. The very man who had driven her kind out of the land was now seeking her counsel, but Saul assured her that no harm would come to her. He just needed to speak to Samuel the prophet. Samuel was dead, by the way. He was the final judge of Israel and a man whose wisdom and privileged connection to God was respected by the people. When Samuel spoke, he spoke the words and will of God. I suspect Saul knew his own doom was nigh. He sought solace—any words of comfort would do. If anyone could console him and offer him hope, it was Samuel. And Saul needed a necromancer to bring Samuel back.

What happened next proves no one should play around with magic arts. Both the witch and Saul got more than they bargained for. Whatever arcane ritual the witch had gone through surprised even her. Whatever invocation she uttered, it worked to the horror of all. A spirit—the ghost of an old man shrouded in a spectral cloak—rose from the ground. It would seem that God deliberately allowed the witch success in her necromancy. God intended to beat Saul at his own game. The text certainly doesn't condone witchcraft, but it does show us that God has *power* over the *powers* of this world. He allowed Samuel's apparition to haunt Saul and announce his ruin. This apparition was no Casper the friendly ghost; he was a grumpy old specter who came to gasp out a final word of disaster. And he wasted no time in challenging Saul.

Samuel gave Saul the same answer he had given him before: "The Lord has turned from you; your kingdom will be taken; your life will be lost." Samuel did not mince words or give Saul false hope. This was no Dickensian Christmas spirit who rattled his chains and gave second chances. There were no words of comfort. There were no further hauntings. There were no opportunities to make amends. The Lord had spoken pronouncements of the end of Saul's kingdom and his right to the kingly succession. This was a bad day for Saul. And it got worse.

First Samuel 31:3-6 gives us the details of Saul's demise in battle a short time later. In the throes of death, after having been pierced by enemy arrows, Saul pleaded with his armor bearer to run him through, lest he fall into enemy hands. Allied soldiers in World War II who faced the Japanese in the Pacific theater would have sympathized with Saul. Better to die, than let the Japanese get their hands on you. Better to die than let those uncircumcised (read: heathen barbarian) Philistines get their meat hooks on you. But there is a stigma with helping your king commit suicide. There is something unsettling about the whole thing. The armor bearer wouldn't do it. So, Saul did it himself. He fell on his sword, thus ending his reign and fulfilling the words spoken through Samuel.

Saul had solicited the powers of mere mortals to change his trajectory. He had played with demonic powers in the hope of turning the tide. He sought answers in places he should not have gone. He attempted to garner God's favor through unfavorable means. Did Saul really think that consulting a necromancer would change the outcomes prescribed by God? Witchcraft and faithful obedience to God are incompatible. The spiritual powers of mediums and necromancers are subject to the God of the universe.

HONEST ANSWERS TO LIFE'S HARDEST QUESTIONS

Two issues arise from the story of Saul and the witch of En-dor. First, how should a believer in God cope with seemingly unanswered prayers? Second, is it acceptable for believers to seek counsel in spiritual sources other than God?

In response to the first issue, God answers prayer in one of two ways: Yes or no. Often the yes or no is also accompanied by a *wait*. Periods of waiting can be blessed opportunities for growth in our faith where God teaches us valuable lessons about ourselves and about his character and actions in this world (1 Pet 1:6–7). Scripture also provides reasons to think that unconfessed sin and rebellion against God might lead to a lack of favorable response (Jas 4:3 and Ps 66:18). We sometimes fail to receive because we ask with improper motives or unconfessed sin. We don't receive because even while confessing belief in God through prayer, we deny him by our actions of disobedience. Saul had rejected God by his defiance and lack of trust. The narrative of the book of 1 Samuel testifies to Saul's disobedience. For that reason, God withdrew his favor and refused Saul the answers he sought.

Prayer is not just about seeking answers to problems. To pray is to commune with God and enjoy fellowship with our creator. God gives us prayer as a gift to be enjoyed. Writing to the Thessalonian church, Paul says, "Rejoice always, pray without ceasing, give thanks in all circumstances; for this is the will of God in Christ Jesus for you" (1 Thess 5:16–18). Prayer redirects our thoughts heavenward and re-aligns our hearts to God. It resituates us and puts us and our problems in their proper context. The blessing of prayer is not just in the answer God provides, but in the fellowship with God that comes from asking.

Regarding the second question, if prayer is honored as stated above, then seeking answers outside of God is moot. If we believe God is who he says he is, if we believe in his revelation through the prophets and apostles, and if we truly believe he is capable of accomplishing the wonders testified to by eyewitnesses and recorded through history, then we have no reason to turn anywhere but to God. Yet, in our impatience, doubt, and desperation, we might turn to anything that promises an answer. In fear we turn to any promise of security, even empty promises.

To turn to witchcraft and magic arts in seeking solutions to life's problems is to forsake the greater power for the lesser. Why seek answers in the created thing, when the Creator is readily available? Why look inward toward a self that lacks both understanding and answers by nature of its physical, mental, and spiritual limitations, when we can look outward toward unlimited wisdom found in God?

Granted, not everyone turns to magic in times of trouble. But magic can take many forms. Often magic is found in temporary solutions to eternal problems. Magic can be anything that promises to assuage our fear, shame, and doubt. Magic might be any ideology or philosophical system that promises answers to our longings and healing from our pain. Sometimes the alleged healing elixir of magic is nothing more than distraction, diversion, and over-indulgence that falsely promises relief. All of these methods might seem to provide solutions, but do they satisfy our deepest needs and longings? The good in these solutions is only as good as the good that comes from the hand of the God who created all good things. The bad is worse than we might imagine; these methods only provide false hope. They do not give us ultimate salvation since there is salvation in no other than Jesus Christ, for there is no other name under heaven by which we can be saved (Acts 4:12).

Saul didn't like what God had to say, so he looked elsewhere. *The truth* wasn't to his liking, so he attempted to live *his truth*. This was an epic fail. But God always has his way of telling us what we need to hear. Furthermore, it seems that Saul wanted to manipulate outcomes. We often do the same, manipulating God's instruction to make it fit a little better into our self-activated prerogatives and priorities. This too is an epic fail. Saul thought he could get divine instruction from someone other than God. In doing this, he sinned. But God showed up anyway and gave him an answer he didn't want. We don't need witches and magic to know God's will. He has given his people Scripture and the Holy Spirit. So, let's bypass the sorcerers, astrologers, mediums, and anyone (or anything) that promises what it can't ultimately deliver. Let's turn to the living God.

STUDY QUESTIONS

1. What experiences have you had with occultic practices or magic arts? How have these encounters affected your relationship with God?

2. Read 1 Samuel 28. How would you define Saul's relationship with God? See also, 1 Samuel 13:8–14 and 15:26–28.

3. At the beginning of 1 Samuel 28, what three means of communication does God withhold from Saul when he makes his inquiry? What is the significance of these? See Exodus 28:30 and Numbers 27:21.

4. Where does Saul turn when he receives no answer from God? How does God use the witch of En-dor to answer Saul? Does the return of the spirit of Samuel teach us anything about the nature of the afterlife? Do you get the impression that the return of deceased people is normal?

5. Is Saul satisfied and comforted in seeking an alternative solution (other than God)? How do Saul's actions dishonor the Lord?

6. In what ways do people look for answers in places other than God's word and prayer? Where do we commonly go when life gets hard?

7. How should we respond to God when we don't get the answers we want at the times we want? See 1 Thessalonians 5:16–18. How have you coped with seemingly unanswered prayer?

1

Valley of Slaughter — 1 Kings 18

So Ahab sent to all the people of Israel and gathered the prophets together at Mount Carmel. And Elijah came near to all the people and said, "How long will you go limping between two different opinions? If the Lord is God, follow him; but if Baal, then follow him." And the people did not answer him a word. Then Elijah said to the people, "I, even I only, am left a prophet of the Lord, but Baal's prophets are 450 men. Let two bulls be given to us, and let them choose one bull for themselves and cut it in pieces and lay it on the wood, but put no fire to it. And I will prepare the other bull and lay it on the wood and put no fire to it. And you call upon the name of your god, and I will call upon the name of the Lord, and the God who answers by fire, he is God." And all the people answered, "It is well spoken." Then Elijah said to the prophets of Baal, "Choose for yourselves one bull and prepare it first, for you are many, and call upon the name of your god, but put no fire to it." And they took the bull that was given them, and they prepared it and called upon the name of Baal from morning until noon, saying, "O Baal, answer us!" But there was no voice, and no one answered. And they limped around the altar that they had made. And at noon Elijah mocked them, saying, "Cry aloud, for he is a god. Either he is musing, or he is relieving himself, or he is on a journey, or perhaps he is asleep and must be awakened." And they cried aloud and cut themselves after their custom with swords and lances, until the blood gushed out upon them. And as midday passed, they raved on until the time of the offering of the oblation, but there was no voice. No one answered;

no one paid attention.

Then Elijah said to all the people, "Come near to me." And all the people came near to him. And he repaired the altar of the Lord that had been thrown down. Elijah took twelve stones, according to the number of the tribes of the sons of Jacob, to whom the word of the Lord came, saying, "Israel shall be your name," and with the stones he built an altar in the name of the Lord. And he made a trench about the altar, as great as would contain two seahs of seed. And he put the wood in order and cut the bull in pieces and laid it on the wood. And he said, "Fill four jars with water and pour it on the burnt offering and on the wood." And he said, "Do it a second time." And they did it a second time. And he said, "Do it a third time." And they did it a third time. And the water ran around the altar and filled the trench also with water.

And at the time of the offering of the oblation, Elijah the prophet came near and said, "O Lord, God of Abraham, Isaac, and Israel, let it be known this day that you are God in Israel, and that I am your servant, and that I have done all these things at your word. Answer me, O Lord, answer me, that this people may know that you, O Lord, are God, and that you have turned their hearts back." Then the fire of the Lord fell and consumed the burnt offering and the wood and the stones and the dust, and licked up the water that was in the trench. And when all the people saw it, they fell on their faces and said, "The Lord, he is God; the Lord, he is God." And Elijah said to them, "Seize the prophets of Baal; let not one of them escape." And they seized them. And Elijah brought them down to the brook Kishon and slaughtered them there.

—I Kings 18:20–40

MANY MIXED MARTIAL ARTS (MMA) fights begin long before the competitors enter the ring. It starts with the weigh in. It heats up at the press conference. It gets real when the two competitors stare each other down and exchange a few choice words, examples of which I can't give you here since this is a Christian book. Sometimes one ugly, tattooed, scar-faced, and testosterone-infused ruffian will be so enraged by the mere sight of his equally ugly, tattooed, and scar-faced opponent that he takes swings at him right there on the platform. At this point, a host of brutes, trainers, and sundry muscle-bound grotesques will jump into the fray and try to take control of the situation before all hell breaks loose and someone gets their gluteus minimus, gluteus medius, and gluteus maximus kicked all at the same time. The fight must wait for the proper place and time. The proper place is the Octagon; the proper time is primetime.

In 1 Kings 18, the Octagon was called Mount Carmel, a site of Baal worship situated directly west of the Sea of Galilee near the Mediterranean and just south of the Phoenician cities of Tyre and Sidon (Jezebel's old stomping ground). The time of the showdown was set for the end of a lengthy drought that had afflicted the land. The opponents where the Canaanite fertility god, Baal, and the one true living God of the Universe, YHWH. These two opponents were represented by Queen Jezebel and her nemesis Elijah. This is made clear in the preceding chapters of 1 Kings where the conflict is introduced. Jezebel hated Elijah and wanted him dead. Everyone knew this. And so, all Israel assembled for the big fight. But this wasn't an MMA beat down. It was a battle of spiritual clout and divine approval. It was a battle to determine which god was real—which god would show up when people beseeched heaven for a fireworks display in the sky. In other words, Elijah's side would pray, and Jezebel's side would also pray, and everyone would wait to see what would happen. Sound boring? Actually, the confrontation was quite dramatic—taunting, name-calling, self-flagellation, fire from heaven, and plenty of death, gore, and carnage. I promise this is better than an MMA fight.

It's hard picturing an old, scrawny, malnourished prophet putting someone in an armbar or roundhouse kicking them in the face. It's also difficult to imagine a regal queen donning boxing shorts and a sports bra and beating the living excrement out of someone else in the ring. Luckily, we don't have to try to imagine either scenario. For one, Jezebel never showed up. Instead, she sent her 450 Baal prophets to the fight. Further, Elijah didn't need to choke hold anyone. Instead, he went into a mild berserker rage, took a sword and butcher the 450 Baal prophets after God appeared in power and proved that Baal is a worthless, impotent, and imaginary god who's about as believable as the Flying Spaghetti Monster.

On the day of the fight, Jezebel's 450 Baal prophets stood on one side of the mountain top, and Elijah stood on the other. The people of Israel crowded around. Vendors sold overpriced beer, nachos, and chilidogs. Images flashed on the jumbotron as announcers hyped up the show. The battle began.

THE HOPELESSNESS OF WISHFUL THINKING

The rules were simple: The Baal prophets and Elijah were each given a bull to sacrifice, both were permitted an opportunity to pray to their god, and whoever's bull spontaneously combusted by divine fire was the winner. With the terms confirmed, Elijah took the microphone, turned to the people, and basically told them to stop riding the fence and being so easily duped into abandoning the true God for Jezebel's fake gods. "How long will you go limping (*pisseh* in Hebrew)," he said. In other words, "How long will you walk in hesitation and indecisiveness like one who wavers foolishly because he is unable to make up his mind. We will soon know which is the true God, and which prophets are dead. Let the battle begin."

With that, the Baal prophets butchered the bull and arranged the pieces on some nice, dry sunbaked firewood mixed with matches, firecrackers, and smoldering cigarette butts. They then prayed and called on Baal in an eclectic mix of Shakespearian and King James English: "Heigh-ho, most fair Baal, thy servants beseech thee to doth rain down heavenly fiery majestic hell on yon tender loin!" They droned on as the crowd rolled their eyes and waited for something interesting to happen. When nothing did, the Baal prophets created some excitement by "limping" (same word as when Elijah addressed the people in verse 21) around the altar and busting out their best breakdancing moves. Baal still didn't show up, but at least the crowd saw some action. As the Baal prophets were moonwalking, popping and locking, and doing that weird horse move from Psy's *Gangnam Style* music video, Elijah taunted them.

To taunt another human being and subject them to public embarrassment is generally considered bad form. Politicians and entertainers frequently engage in this kind of childishness. It serves as publicity for them, while creating fodder for the media. Celebrity mudslinging and feuds serve as lowbrow entertainment. However, in the situation of 1 Kings 18, the absurdity of the Baal prophets' spectacle can't be ignored. They were asking for it. Elijah gave it to them: "Maybe he is musing—contemplating the origin of the universe or the meaning of life. Maybe he's on the toilet and suffering from a bad case of constipation. Send him a few laxatives and see if that speeds things up. Maybe the loo is clogged and he can't find the plunger. Maybe he's on vacation and isn't checking texts and emails. Maybe he's sleeping off last night's binge and he just needs a cup of coffee. The poor guy needs some help. Pray louder!"

At this, the Baal prophets went into a greater fury than before. Desperate, they cut and beat themselves until the time of the evening sacrifice. Still nothing. Baal ran out of toilet paper and no one was within ear shot to come to his rescue. So finally, while Baal sat helpless on the can, the Baal prophets gave up.

Next up, Elijah shows everyone what it looks like to put complete trust in the power of God. Elijah truly believed that God is exactly who he says he is. The prophet ensured no one would leave with any questions in their mind. He sabotaged his own altar, making it impossible for any earthly fire to consume his sacrifice. After cutting up his sacrificial bull, he placed it on an altar of twelve stones, representing the twelve tribes of Israel with whom God had made his covenant promise to bless and redeem. He soaked the altar with water. Then he soaked it again. After that, he made sure to soak it one last time for good measure. Now that it was impossible (or highly improbable) for a fire to light the altar, he prayed once to the Lord and asked that God show his power to the people he had called, loved, set apart, and saved.

God answered with a radiant ball of napalm from the sky. In a blazing display of divine power, the bull, the wood, the altar, and the water were vaporized, discrediting Baal in a public and embarrassing display.[1] He crumpled in the first round, after taking one punch to the face. Jezebel and her prophets lost. Elijah won. The victor was undisputed. To celebrate, Elijah rounded up the Baal prophets and took them down to the Kishon Valley, where the Kishon River flows west and empties into the Mediterranean Sea. Elijah then slaughtered the prophets of Baal, finishing the violent and self-destructive job they started.[2]

I actually have it on good authority that in a lost interview for *Rolling Stone*, Elijah was asked about incident: "What happened that day on Mount Carmel?" He simply looked grimly at the interviewer and quoted Conan the Barbarian: "Crush your enemies, see them driven before you, hear the lamentation of the women." He then stood up and walked out of the interview.

---

1. Commentator, Dale Ralph Davis, argues that Baal had to be publicly discredited prior to God sending rain, lest the people attribute the rain storm mentioned in 1 Kings 18:41–46 to Baal rather than YHWH. See Davis, *1 Kings*, 227.

2. The text isn't clear about whose hand wielded the weapon of judgment. Nor is it clear what instrument was used to put the Baal prophets to death. What is clear is that Elijah was the instigator of the judgment and that the people aided him in the task.

The slaughter of the Baal prophets at the hand of Elijah should not shock us. The sin of idolatry leads to inner spiritual death that leads to eternal death. Those who lead others into such sin are doubly guilty of destruction. Jesus himself said that whoever causes one who believes in him to sin, it would be better for that person to have a great millstone fastened around his neck and to be drowned in the depth of the sea (Matt 18:6). That's pretty brutal. The prophets of Baal had conspired with Jezebel to lead God's people astray. Idolatry was a deliberate mockery of the God who had delivered the people of Israel from bondage in Egypt. To abandon the living God for a false god made of stone is like skipping out on an all-inclusive tropical vacation for an at-home staring contest with a shabby pixelated photo of a beach. We can't explain the insanity of idolatry or excuse the insult it is to the true and living God. It's just plain dumb. But in our stupidity, we all do it. Every time God offers us a path to an abundant life, we go our way, and suffer.

We, like the Baal prophets, like to do things the hard way. Baal's servants made fools of themselves. Elijah merely pointed out the obvious. Given the opportunity, we might have joined these fools in their spectacle. But praise be to the God of grace; he has delivered his people in love and restored us in mercy (Eph 1:3–14).

A FAITH THAT AIMS AT TRUTH

We learn three important lessons about faith from the story of Elijah and the Baal prophets. First, faith is not an irrational leap into the darkness. It is a rational, cognitive attitude that aims at truth and pursues the truth. Both religious skeptics and religious believers have wrongly defined faith as a mere guess—a desperate and irrational cognitive lunge toward what they hope is true. Philosopher, Peter Boghossian, defined faith (wrongly) as "belief without evidence" and "pretending to know things you don't know."[3] Faith of this kind is reduced to wishful thinking, positive thinking, or self-manipulation into believing something regardless of evidential or rational support. This isn't the biblical definition of faith; I don't know one serious Christian thinker who defines faith this way. But it's easier to claim faith is irrational nonsense, and then pat ourselves on the back for poking holes in that apparent nonsense. Hebrews 11:1 tells us that "faith is the assurance of things hoped for, the conviction of things not seen." Notice that the author

3. Boghossian, *Manual for Creating Atheists*, 21.

of Hebrews uses the language of cognition and trust. Faith is an epistemic term. It has to do with confident belief. This doesn't negate the importance of other factors that cooperate with faith and play a role in our understanding of the world. The Bible doesn't separate faith from things such as truth, fact, evidence, justification, reason, warrant, reality, perception, or any other concept central to knowledge acquisition. God's actions, his natural and scriptural revelation, and his fulfillment of promises provide reasons to adopt a cognitive attitude of faith.

It wasn't faith, but folly, that drove the Baal prophets. Wishful thinking characterized the belief system of the Baal prophets and their followers. Baal, the fertility god of the Canaanites, failed to pour rain on the land (1 Kgs 18:1). Nor could he ignite fire. He couldn't even muster the power to show up and apologize to his followers for his failings. Ironically, his silence was proof of the fertility god's impotence. On the contrary, it's not folly to trust in a God who sends fire and rain, and who speaks truth to his servants. True faith is based on the truths of who God says he is and on the reality of what God has done. Faith is a step into the glorious light of truth.

Second, the object of our faith matters more than our perceived amount of faith. The Baal prophets thought if they closed their eyes, clenched their fists, and repeated, "I believe I can fly," over and over, they would take off into the air. This is not biblical faith. Yet this is the image many have of Christian belief. We think lengthy prayers will make us holier in the sight of heaven. Similarly, we imagine the multiplication of spiritual blather will elicit a more favorable response from God (Matt 6:7). We forget that quality intentional time in the Bible will often produce better results than long distracted readings of Scripture. We forsake active listening and the use of few carefully chosen words when speaking to others, and opt for impassioned off-putting discourses. More is not necessarily better. To possess faith the size of a mustard seed means quality over quantity (Matt 17:20–1). *Modest* faith in the one true God means far more than *considerable* faith in a false one.

Third, the Christian faith is not substantiated by popular opinion, but by its relationship to the truth. Baal had 450 prophets present on Mount Carmel. He had King Ahab and Queen Jezebel on his side. He had multitudes who lacked the courage or decisiveness to deny him and put their faith in the true God. The numbers were in his favor. Numbers, however, didn't make him any more real. Numbers didn't afford him greater power or authority. Numbers failed to bring victory. Regardless of what the media tells us, truth is not determined by popular opinion, angry crowds, and vitriolic social media posts.

Like the people of Israel in ancient times, God's church today often "limps" between two positions. We speak of faith but lack it. We speak of truth but deny it. We trust in ourselves, our instincts, and our resources to help us, and cry out to God only when all other measures fail to come through. God becomes an afterthought. Let's pause and ask: In what areas have we wavered between God and the world. In what areas have we ridden the fence and failed to follow God with an undivided heart? In what ways have we failed to acknowledge the sufficiency of the sacrifice of Jesus Christ in restoring us from death to life and in healing our shame, guilt, and fear?

STUDY QUESTIONS

1. When you pray, do you expect God to answer? Do you think there are ways of praying that will make God more likely respond? Explain.

2. Read 1 Kings 18:20–40 and summarize the story. Who are the main characters?

3. What test does Elijah call for to evaluate which is the true God? How do the Baal prophets perform in the test?

4. What does Elijah do to his sacrifice? Why is it important that he soaks the offering?

5. What does this passage teach us about the nature of God?

6. Is it right and just that Elijah puts the Baal prophets to the sword? Read Exodus 20:3–6 and Deuteronomy 17:2–7.

7. What does the test between Elijah and the Baal prophets teach us about the nature of faith? What is faith? How much faith should a person have? How does faith relate to truth?

8. Why does faith in Jesus and what he accomplished at the cross matter for us?

8

Rotten Bowels — 2 Chronicles 21

When Jehoram had ascended the throne of his father and was established, he killed all his brothers with the sword, and also some of the princes of Israel. Jehoram was thirty-two years old when he became king, and he reigned eight years in Jerusalem. And he walked in the way of the kings of Israel, as the house of Ahab had done, for the daughter of Ahab was his wife. And he did what was evil in the sight of the Lord. Yet the Lord was not willing to destroy the house of David, because of the covenant that he had made with David, and since he had promised to give a lamp to him and to his sons forever.

—2 Chronicles 21:4–7

Moreover, he [Jehoram] made high places in the hill country of Judah and led the inhabitants of Jerusalem into whoredom and made Judah go astray. And a letter came to him from Elijah the prophet, saying, "Thus says the Lord, the God of David your father, 'Because you have not walked in the ways of Jehoshaphat your father, or in the ways of Asa king of Judah, but have walked in the way of the kings of Israel and have enticed Judah and the inhabitants of Jerusalem into whoredom, as the house of Ahab led Israel into whoredom, and also you have killed your brothers, of your father's house, who were better than you, behold, the Lord will bring a great plague on your people, your children, your wives, and all your possessions, and you yourself will have a severe sickness with a disease of your bowels, until your bowels come out because of the disease, day by day."

—2 Chronicles 21:11–15

And after all this the Lord struck him in his bowels with an incurable disease. In the course of time, at the end of two years, his bowels came out because of the disease, and he died in great agony. His people made no fire in his honor, like the fires made for his fathers. He was thirty-two years old when he began to reign, and he reigned eight years in Jerusalem. And he departed with no one's regret. They buried him in the city of David, but not in the tombs of the kings.

—2 Chronicles 21:18–20

KING JEHORAM WILL ALWAYS be remembered as the king whose intestines fell out of his body. A quick internet search on the average length of the human intestine (small and large combined) reveals mixed results. As I scrolled through the data, I found varying averages and can't provide an accurate answer. Nine feet. Fourteen feet. Eighteen feet. Twenty-two feet. The most legitimate peer-reviewed article I found claimed a whopping twenty-six feet.[1] You would think someone could figure this out. However, since this isn't an academic research paper, let's just say the average human intestine is somewhere between one and fifty feet. Does that sound fair? It's close enough for our intended purposes, and it's as good as anything you'll find on the internet.

Intestines are important in breaking down and absorbing nutrients from food and water.[2] They are also tremendous producers of methane gas and feces. But you knew that already. Human intestines work hard each and every day, especially in America where we overload on junk food and

1. I had to dig into some heavy-duty academic research to get at the truth of the matter. A 2002 paper on the subject contained the following data acquired from a study: "Two hundred non-fixed adult cadavers (100 men, 100 women) who willingly gave their bodies for scientific purposes were studied. The postmortem average length of the whole intestine was 795.5±129cm and was significantly longer in men and in young subjects." Hounnou, *et al.* "Anatomical Study of Human Intestine," 24, 290–94. Voila, twenty-six feet of intestine.

2. The Mayo Clinic website provides plenty of nifty facts and images in case anyone cares. https://www.mayoclinic.org/colon-and-small-intestine/img-20008226.

then stress our poor bowels with crash diets. A lot can go wrong with the digestive tract from the moment food enters the mouth to the moment it exits the rectum. Inflammatory bowel disease sounds particularly uncomfortable. Irritable bowel syndrome sounds bothersome and potentially embarrassing. Constipation. Diarrhea. Dysentery. The list goes on. As an interesting random historical anecdote, King Louis XIV was apparently a frequent recipient of enemas for the cleansing of the bowels. But let the reader understand, I draw attention to these facts only because intestine-related discussions play an important part of both human physiology and biblical history. Let the reader understand.

Most people are familiar with the Judas Iscariot intestine story from Acts 1:18 (see the chapter *Grizzly Suicide*). Fewer people are aware of the King Jehoram intestine story from 2 Chronicles 21. These two men have much in common. Both of them were scoundrels. Both failed to live up to the great responsibility of their calling. Both of them lost their intestines. And when I say lost, I mean lost. Their intestines literally fell out of their bodies. It's gross. It's distasteful. It's irreverent. But it's in the Bible; if we are to value and understand the word of God, we need to deal with this episode and learn what we can from it.

It would seem Jehoram suffered from a prolapse of the intestines. In layman's terms, his innards departed his body through the rectum. In middle-school boys' terms, he farted really hard, and his entire digestive tract fell out. No doubt, his death, and the sickness leading up to it, was accompanied by great anguish. Jehoram sinned grievously against God and against God's beloved people. For this, the Lord struck him down and he died.

We're told no one grieved over the loss. No one honored the fallen king. He was deprived of a king's burial. He was neither missed nor mourned. No one cared. No one showed up at the funeral. No flags were flown at half-mast. No pint glasses were raised in his honor. No songs of glory were sung. His body was thrown in a common grave and it seems unlikely anyone attended the wake, even though they were serving free hors-d'oeuvres. His legacy was one of idolatry, whoredom, pain, and godlessness—leading the people of Israel to lust after the gods and the practices of the Canaanites and inciting the people to commit egregious sins against the true God (2 Chr 21:11). He was a murderer of his own people and of his own family members (2 Chr 21:4). He was a jerk—the son of a motherless goat. He was *stoopid* with two o's. The irony of this story is not lost on commentator,

Matthew Henry, who notes: "Jehoram, whose heart was wicked, was struck in his inwards, and he that had no bowels of compassion towards his brethren was so plagued in his bowels that they fell out."[3] The seat of the emotions and thoughts in Hebrew culture was the bowels. In modern language, we might say the king lacked a heart for God and his people, and God struck him with a heart attack. Either way, Jehoram left behind a heritage of rotten entrails and little more. What will we leave?

A DEATH UNOBSERVED

One day, Jehoram sat in his palace in Jerusalem, thinking how to encourage Baal worship throughout his kingdom, while enjoying a nice lunch and the performances of the court jugglers, and dancing girls. As he finished the last bite of his Philly cheesesteak, his stomach rumbled. He tried Tums. He tried Pepto-Bismol. Nothing quelled the agitation he experienced. It only worsened. This was the beginning of the end.

At that moment, his royal courier burst into the room with a letter from the prophet Elijah. It was addressed to the king. As the herald read the letter, the list of grievances was laid bare. The king's evil had not been lost on the Lord. Jehoram would pay for his sin. But then came the final lines of Elijah's letter—words of woe, words of doom. "You will be afflicted with a painful disease of the bowels. It will start with rumblings and tremblings, followed by inflammation and burning, proceeded by painful belching, gulping, and tidal waves of hemorrhoidal discomfort. Then when you think it can't get worse, agonizing prolapsus of the entrails will ensue. Your bowels will exit your body. You will try to stuff them back in but to no avail. You will look down in disbelief as you realize that your *innards* are now your *outtards*. You will gasp out your last breath in utter agony as you crumple to the floor, a hollow shell of a man." I obviously took the liberty of embellishing the retelling. But the main idea is that God judged, and Jehoram died.

The gruesomeness of the death can easily overshadow other important moral and theological aspects of the story. In fact, the manner of Jehoram's death might distract us from how despicable he was in life, and how quickly he was forgotten. The central message of this biblical episode is not that Jehoram died, but that no one mourned him. This offers us an opportunity for introspection. How we will be remembered? Will we have given anyone reason to mourn our passing? How will our life have influenced those

3. Henry, *Commentary on the Whole Bible*, 598.

around us? What will we have done with the precious time God has given us? Will we have sought out opportunities to speak words of comfort and care to those in need? Will we have given of our time, our resources, and our very selves? Will we have recognized the most important things in life? Will we have placed such high priority on the things of God that all who knew us would speak of our faith, love, and integrity?

Some people sow little more than heartbreak, neglect, and abandonment. Others leave a legacy of pain and abuse. Still others leave their debt for the bereaved to clear up. Jehoram left behind two things: A broken kingdom and a pile of reeking intestines. He led the people away from God. He encouraged ruined people to cherish their ruin and nurture further ruin. He urged sinners to enjoy their sin. He fostered rebellion against God—rebellion that would only reap judgment. He harmed those who desperately needed a gentle guiding hand. He was irresponsible with the calling God had placed on him to reflect the Lord's kingship in humility and love. He married wicked Athaliah, daughter of wicked Jezebel, wicked queen of the wicked kingdom of Israel (2 Kgs 11).

Many have family members who left a tarnished legacy. Fathers who ignored their children. Mothers who showed favoritism. Relatives who belittled and overlooked us in our moments of need. Abusive uncles. Bitter grandmothers. Alcoholic parents. Guardians who failed to guard us. Friends who let us down. People who contributed little positivity to a world plagued with too much negativity.

Hopefully, we can also point to examples of love and tenderness. Those who mentor, teach, support, and listen. Those who invest in us and make us better humans. These are people who understand the value of passing on wisdom to the next generation. They show up. They apply themselves to the betterment of others. There's warmth in their eyes and kindness in their words. Even their rebuke makes us better. We welcome their accountability. They view the world through an eternal lens and understand that they live for much more than a fleeting moment. Their palpable love for God and pervading faith leaves no question to the transformative work of Christ in their hearts. Even amidst struggle and pain, they exude genuine devotion. They are honest about their sin, and genuine in their repentance. These are people who are truly mourned when they die.

A LEGACY OF HOPE

Jehoram was quickly and intentionally forgotten. That should give us pause. Who will remember us? How will they remember us? Inevitably, those we leave behind will forget us with time. After all, how many of us can remember the names of our great grandparents, let alone our long dead ancestors? Our names will be forgotten, but the impact we have in others' lives may linger far beyond what we can anticipate. Before we ask ourselves how we will be remembered, let's reorient ourselves as *rememberers*. We want to be remembered as people who remember. How we are remembered has everything to do with our own commitment to remember the most important things—who God is and what he has done. Don't seek to leave a great legacy; instead, seek to remember Jesus Christ and let the gospel transform your life. If you want to be remembered for the right reasons, then remember your Creator, Savior, and Lord (Ecc 12:1).

Jesus instituted communion (the Lord's Supper) as a way for the church to remember his sacrifice, his love, and his covenant of grace (1 Cor 11:23–26). Remembering Jesus is central to a life of devotion and obedience. It happens in prayer and study of the word, through active participation in the mission of Jesus Christ to engage the world and those who suffer in it. Remembering happens when the Spirit of God realigns our hearts to Christ. How we are remembered by others has everything to do with our remembrance of Christ as we elevate him to a place of supremacy in our lives. Whether we are loved for our Christian devotion, or hated for it, let's at least not be ignored. The world should know what we believe, and they should see the good fruit of that belief in our lives.

The saddest lines of 2 Chronicles 21 are the words: "He departed with no one's regret." Will people joyfully exclaim, "good riddance," at our death, or will they remember what we brought to their lives? In the story of Jehoram's tragic death there is a lesson: Seek the Lord with all your heart (or bowels). Love the Lord with all your might. Believe Jesus. Trust him. Love your neighbor. Care for those God brings into your life. Nurture your children and hear them when they talk. Speak a loving word to your spouse. Show up. Stick around. Turn off the distractions. Notice those who need to be noticed. Let the gospel of grace be at the center of who you are.

STUDY QUESTIONS

1. How do you want to be remembered? How might this differ from how people might actually remember you?

2. Read 2 Chronicles 21:1–20. What kind of man was Jehoram? What were his crimes (sins) against God and the law? How did his sin affect those who lived under his reign?

3. What was the punishment for Jehoram's crimes? Is there any significance to the kind of punishment Jehoram received?

4. Who delivered the bad news? Is there any significance to God's choice of messenger who brought this news to the king?

5. What was the reaction of the people when Jehoram died? Think of the reactions you have when various politicians leave office or when a boss resigns from work. Can you relate to the indifference/relief of the people of Israel under Jehoram?

6. What does this story teach us about the importance of the impact we can make in the lives of those around us? If you were to die today, who would show up at your funeral? Who do you want at your funeral and what reasons are you giving them to show up?

9

Gruesome Annihilation — Joshua 6

On the seventh day they rose early, at the dawn of day, and marched around the city in the same manner seven times. It was only on that day that they marched around the city seven times. And at the seventh time, when the priests had blown the trumpets, Joshua said to the people, "Shout, for the Lord has given you the city. And the city and all that is within it shall be devoted to the Lord for destruction. Only Rahab the prostitute and all who are with her in her house shall live, because she hid the messengers whom we sent. But you, keep yourselves from the things devoted to destruction, lest when you have devoted them you take any of the devoted things and make the camp of Israel a thing for destruction and bring trouble upon it. But all silver and gold, and every vessel of bronze and iron, are holy to the Lord; they shall go into the treasury of the Lord." So the people shouted, and the trumpets were blown. As soon as the people heard the sound of the trumpet, the people shouted a great shout, and the wall fell down flat, so that the people went up into the city, every man straight before him, and they captured the city. Then they devoted all in the city to destruction, both men and women, young and old, oxen, sheep, and donkeys, with the edge of the sword.

—*J*OSHUA *6:15–21*

IT'S IN OUR NATURE to want to knock things over. Remember when you were a kid and some neighborhood kid built a snow fort or snowman? It would stand there tempting you to knock it down. A few times in my life, the temptation was too much to bear. I had to act. I had to knock it over, practice my swordsmanship on it with a stick, or stomp it out of existence.

Similarly, I remember times when I would build a snowman. My friends and siblings spent hours of excruciating Sisyphean labor rolling heavy, wet snow into balls. Even after all that work, we would immediately unleash hell on the army of snowmen we'd built. Knocking things over is fun.

Have you seen footage of failed building demolitions? A crowd gathers to watch as the explosive charges fire one by one. Everyone holds their breath, waiting for the condemned structure to tumble to the ground in a cloud of smoke and debris. But there's no collapse, no debris, no celebration of mayhem and destruction, because some amateur set the explosives in the wrong place. What a disappointment. People pay good money to watch mayhem and destruction.

Anyway, here's where I'm going with this: The walls of Jericho needed to come down. And do you know who's good at building demolition? God. Sometimes he knocks things over. And when he does, the results are spectacular. As the perfect omniscient engineer of the universe, he knows how to put things together, and how to take them apart. One of his best demo jobs occurred at Jericho, a Canaanite city located a few miles west of the Jordan river. Jericho was the first major town on the path to Israelite conquest of the promised land. It had to be destroyed. So, God showed up and made the wall collapse. He didn't even use explosives. It was terrific. He simply told some crazy blokes to walk around the city seven times and then shout really loud and play some jazz on their trumpets and saxophones. Frightened by this spectacle, the wall gave up and keeled over in a pile of rubble and blood. Back in those days the Israelites didn't have tanks and helicopters. They didn't even have catapults, cannons, or blunderbusses. If they wanted to conquer a walled city, they had few options. You could tunnel under the wall, you could build a siege ramp, or you could starve out the inhabitants. Or God could knock it over and save you the trouble.

According to the *World History Encyclopedia*, Jericho was among the first walled cities in the world.[1] Both *The Archeologist* and the *World Atlas* go further and actually give the honors of oldest walled city to Jericho, hands down.[2] Evidence of human settlement at Jericho dates back as far as

1. Mark, "Ancient City."
2. See "Ancient Jericho" at Archaeologist.org and "City of Jericho" at WorldAtlas.

8000 BC. As agriculture developed and people created permanent towns, walls became necessary for the prevention of attack by roving bands of nomads, migrant tribes, and soccer hooligans. Jericho's regional prominence made it a logical target for Israel's first strike on the land of Canaan. Imagine the *honor* of partnering with God to knock down the oldest wall in the world. Imagine the *horror* of being tasked with the slaughter of every man, woman, and child behind that wall.

It's not unreasonable to ask why God would be so brutal in his dealings with the inhabitants of Jericho. Is God a genocidal maniac who delights in the wanton slaughter of children? Was Joshua, the God-anointed leader of Israel, an unfeeling Terminator who was hell-bent on destroying everything in his path until the mission was accomplished? Like a stoic, unfeeling, heavily muscled cybernetic organism, wearing a leather jacket and sunglasses, and armed with a M134 minigun, did Joshua march into Jericho and annihilate his enemies? It seems pretty darn brutal if you ask me. Even the animals were put to death: Oxen, sheep, donkeys, cats, dogs, and gerbils. The goldfish were all flushed down the toilet, and the cockroaches were stomped to death. Nothing survived. What are we to make of this? Is the God of love, whom we read about all over the Bible, the same God who showed up to kick the rear ends of some nice happy people in a nice little city?

DEVOTED TO DESTRUCTION

The people of Israel aimlessly wandered in the Sinai desert for forty years as punishment for their excessive grumbling and lack of faith. Finally, God told them to enter the land he had promised to their forefathers. They would take possession of the land of Canaan—a land flowing with milk and honey (Exod 3:8). This was easier said than done. A nation of tens of thousands had to first cross the Jordan River, drive out the inhabitants of the land, also numbering tens of thousands, and resettle the land after distributing it according to their tribes and clans. The inhabitants of the land didn't want

---

com. A few scholars take issue with the biblical account of Jericho's collapse. Peter Enns, in *Bible Tells Me So*, questions whether there was even a walled settlement at Jericho when the Israelites were thought to have moved through the area. But then again, Peter Enns questions just about everything in the Bible. There are things about ancient history we will struggle to know with certainty. But on this issue, I'll take my stand with the biblical account.

to give up their homes, for obvious reasons. This meant there would be an inevitable clash of nations.

To prepare for the invasion, Joshua, the leader of the Israelites, sent spies into the land to see what they were up against. As noted previously, Jericho, a fortified city west of the Jordan, was the first strategic target. A successful operation required stealth. So, the two spies went to a local costume shop to buy disguises. Dressed as Darth Vadar and a T-Rex, they slipped past the guards unnoticed and spent the day looking around for a good place to plant a bomb. After taking careful notes on Jericho's defenses, it would seem the two spies stopped off at the local gentlemen's club for some refreshment and entertainment. There, they met a stripper named Rahab. She took notice of the oddly dressed strangers, and when her shift ended, she sat down for a drink and some chitchat.

A few notes on Rahab: First, some argue "prostitute" may have meant anything from unmarried woman to bar wench, but the most natural reading of the text is that Rahab was a *bona fide* strumpet, in the truest sense of the word—lush of hip, heavy of breast, and well acquainted with the ways of carnal pleasure.[3]

Second, it does not appear that the spies solicited her services, though we can't be entirely sure. The Jewish spies knew the laws of Israel and the trouble they could get into for such an indiscretion, especially given the high stakes at the time and their renewed vows to God and celebration of the Passover. It's unlikely they fraternized this way with a vile, heathen people they were only coming back to destroy days later. As travelers seeking refuge, it's plausible they met Rahab at an inn (or her home) where they needed lodging.

Third, it seems Rahab had heard of the fame of the God of Israel. She showed tremendous faith in not only speaking to the spies, but in housing them, and ultimately facilitating their escape. Finally, note that Rahab and her family were the sole survivors of the fall of Jericho. She was spared for her cooperation with the spies. In fact, Rahab shows up in the genealogy of Jesus in Matthew 1:5, and as an example of faith in Hebrews 11:31 and James 2:25. I guess she turned out okay in the end.

The rest of Jericho did not. The spies made their escape, reported back to General Joshua, and the troops were mustered for an attack. Like Clark Griswald leading his family on a transcontinental journey to Wally World with unswerving zeal, Joshua led the Israelites straight into the gaping maw

3. For further discussion of this matter, see Hess, *Joshua*, 83.

of the enemy. When the wall collapsed by the power of God, the Israelite army entered the city and put to the sword all living things found within it. Armed with scythes, rakes, and water balloon launchers, and seething with elemental fury, this mob of desert rustics finally got to see some action.

Now, let's pause to let the ornery naysayer and religious skeptic give their two cents about how *technically* Rahab's house was part of the wall (Josh 2:15), and how *technically* if the wall collapsed she couldn't have survived, and how "see I told you the Bible contradicts itself and doesn't make any sense . . . so there!" Fair enough. But maybe a God who is capable of destroying a city wall is also capable of leaving a small section of it intact. The point is that Rahab and her family somehow survived while the rest of the city was devoted to destruction.

Besides killing everyone in Jericho, the Israelite army was to loot all the gold, silver, and precious articles from the city. They plundered the bling, the iPhones, and the collections of vintage vinyl. They swiped the children's video game consoles and Transformers action figures, along with all the fancy espresso machines. They burned everything else.

The whole affair was pretty brutal if you ask me. What are we to make of God's brutality? Whenever we read a passage of Scripture, one of the most important questions we can ask is: What does this passage tell us about God? Well, what does Joshua 6 tell us about God? A cursory reading tells us he killed a whole lot of people. If we were to ask the infamous atheist apologist Richard Dawkins what Joshua 6 tells us about God, he would say:

> The God of the Old Testament is arguably the most unpleasant character in all fiction: jealous and proud of it; a petty, unjust, unforgiving control-freak; a vindictive, bloodthirsty ethnic cleanser; a misogynistic, homophobic, racist, infanticidal, genocidal, filicidal, pestilential, megalomaniacal, sadomasochistic, capaciously malevolent bully.[4]

But there's more to the story. Look deeper.

GENOCIDE OR JUDGMENT

To better grasp what's going on in Joshua 6, we need to understand who God is. We need to also understand who God is in context to who the Canaanites were. So, let's review a few important aspects of God's character.

4. Dawkins, *God Delusion*, 31.

God is holy. He is other. He is set apart from the world and its sin. His glory and majesty is set above everything contaminated by evil. God is also just. He repays good with good. He judges evil and ultimately restores those who cry out for mercy and who repent and turn to him in faith. In addition, God is patient. For over 400 years, God allowed the sins of the Canaanites to fester and reach their full measure before exacting judgment on them (Gen 15:16). Imagine 400 years of patiently watching the world go to hell in complete disregard for the moral code implanted in its heart (Rom 1:18–20). Can any of us claim such patience? To my fault, I often become frustrated and annoyed with my children quickly and unjustly over minor offenses. I lose my mind after five minutes. It takes God years to get angry. To allow absolute moral filth to accumulate for 400 years shows great forbearance on his part.

God, in his mercy, gave the Canaanites ample warning. Joshua 5:1 says the people of Canaan heard the Israelites were coming, that God had dried up the Jordan River before them, and their "hearts melted and there was no longer any spirit in them." In other words, they collectively pooped their pants when they heard Israel was on their doorstep. The Canaanites had heard of the fame of the God of Israel who defeated the Egyptians and parted the Red Sea. This was a God who had provided his people with manna in the wilderness for decades. When YHWH showed up in Canaan, the inhabitants should have gotten the hint and fled. In fact, it's likely most non-combatants would have left Jericho before Joshua showed up. Like in any good Hollywood western, when the outlaws arrive in town, people board the windows, load the wagons, and anyone who doesn't want to stick around for the showdown gets "the hell out of Dodge." Think: *High Noon*. Think: *Open Range*. It's possible that a few women and children were killed at Jericho. It's doubtful the carnage was as bad as we might imagine. God is just, but he's never a monster.

This was a takeover, not a genocide. The goal was not to wipe the Canaanites from the face of the earth because of their ethnic origins. Israel was used by God to judge the Canaanites through war and to drive them out of the land. This was different from the episodes of ethnic cleansing we might imagine today (Nazi Germany and the Rwandan Genocide). After-all, Rahab and her family, Canaanites by ethnicity, were spared. We read later in Joshua 9 that the Gibeonites were spared through an alliance with Joshua. Even the Israelites themselves were an ethnically diverse group, having intermarried with various other groups. Moses is a prime example;

he married a Cushite, or Ethiopian woman (Num 12:1). The violence of Jericho is about judgment, not genocide.

Who God is and who the Canaanites were is vital to a clear and honest reading of Joshua 6. We've looked at God's character, but who were the Canaanites? We get a glimpse into their lives by understanding the kind of gods they worshipped. Chief among their deities was Baal, a fertility god who sent rain on the earth when his worshippers engaged in ritual sex. Baal's consort was Anath, a bloodthirsty goddess of war and sex. In her bloodlust, she's depicted as having decorated herself with severed human heads.[5] This is a far cry from the God of Israel who promised to prosper his people and bless the nations through them (Gen 22:18).

The crimes of the Canaanites included all kinds of illicit, adulterous, incestuous, and sexually perverse acts.[6] According to biblical historians, bestiality was also common among the Canaanites.[7] This might explain why even the animals of Jericho were put to death. It seems as if nothing had been left untainted by the moral corruption of the people. The poison of sin had filtered down through every level of Canaanite society. Until we come to grasp the depravity of humans and the goodness of God, we can't understand the justice of the destruction of Jericho.

It is not wrong, odd, or outrageous that a perfectly good and holy God would judge a perfectly vile and corrupt people. What God did to the Canaanites in judgment of sin fits squarely within his prerogatives and character. Likewise, what God did at the cross, where Jesus, the second member of the triune godhead, died a painful and humiliating death, on behalf of a vile and corrupt people fits squarely with his prerogatives and character. According to God's justice, some will be rightly condemned. Likewise, according to God's justice, some will receive the righteousness of Christ and be saved. In either case, God comes out right in the end.

5. See Copan, *Is God a Moral Monster*, 159–60.

6. Ibid., 159.

7. Ibid., 159.

STUDY QUESTIONS

1. Have you ever viewed God as cruel and inhumane? Explain.

2. Read Joshua 6. Summarize the story in your own words.

3. What commands does God give Joshua concerning the pre-battle, battle, and post-battle? Is there any significance to marching around the city for seven days? What role does the arch of the covenant play in the battle? Who is the hero of the story?

4. Do you think God was too harsh with the inhabitants of Jericho in ordering their annihilation? Who were the inhabitants of Jericho, and what crimes do you think they had committed against God? See Deuteronomy 20:16–18.

5. Where do we see God's mercy in this story? Who was Rahab and why was she spared? See Joshua 2, Matthew 1:5, and Hebrews 11:31.

6. Can the story of Joshua and the battle of Jericho be used to justify religious wars today? What might have made the Canaanite conquest a unique incident in history?

7. Do you identify more with Joshua and the army of Israel, or with Jericho and the Canaanites?

8. Based on the sacrificial death of Jesus for our sin, how do you suppose God would deal with Jericho today?

10

Dismembered Concubine — Judges 19

In those days, when there was no king in Israel, a certain Levite was sojourning in the remote parts of the hill country of Ephraim, who took to himself a concubine from Bethlehem in Judah. And his concubine was unfaithful to him, and she went away from him to her father's house at Bethlehem in Judah, and was there some four months. Then her husband arose and went after her, to speak kindly to her and bring her back. He had with him his servant and a couple of donkeys. And she brought him into her father's house. And when the girl's father saw him, he came with joy to meet him. And his father-in-law, the girl's father, made him stay, and he remained with him three days. So they ate and drank and spent the night there. And on the fourth day they arose early in the morning, and he prepared to go, but the girl's father said to his son-in-law, "Strengthen your heart with a morsel of bread, and after that you may go." So the two of them sat and ate and drank together. And the girl's father said to the man, "Be pleased to spend the night, and let your heart be merry." And when the man rose up to go, his father-in-law pressed him, till he spent the night there again. And on the fifth day he arose early in the morning to depart. And the girl's father said, "Strengthen your heart and wait until the day declines." So they ate, both of them. And when the man and his concubine and his servant rose up to depart, his father-in-law, the girl's father, said to him, "Behold, now the day has waned toward evening. Please, spend the night. Behold, the day draws to its close. Lodge here and let your heart be merry, and tomorrow you shall arise early in the morning for your journey, and go home."

But the man would not spend the night. He rose up and departed and arrived opposite Jebus (that is, Jerusalem). He had with him a couple of saddled donkeys, and his concubine was with him. When they were near Jebus, the day was nearly over, and the servant said to his master, "Come now, let us turn aside to this city of the Jebusites and spend the night in it." And his master said to him, "We will not turn aside into the city of foreigners, who do not belong to the people of Israel, but we will pass on to Gibeah." And he said to his young man, "Come and let us draw near to one of these places and spend the night at Gibeah or at Ramah." So they passed on and went their way. And the sun went down on them near Gibeah, which belongs to Benjamin, and they turned aside there, to go in and spend the night at Gibeah. And he went in and sat down in the open square of the city, for no one took them into his house to spend the night.

And behold, an old man was coming from his work in the field at evening. The man was from the hill country of Ephraim, and he was sojourning in Gibeah. The men of the place were Benjaminites. And he lifted up his eyes and saw the traveler in the open square of the city. And the old man said, "Where are you going? And where do you come from?" And he said to him, "We are passing from Bethlehem in Judah to the remote parts of the hill country of Ephraim, from which I come. I went to Bethlehem in Judah, and I am going to the house of the Lord, but no one has taken me into his house. We have straw and feed for our donkeys, with bread and wine for me and your female servant and the young man with your servants. There is no lack of anything." And the old man said, "Peace be to you; I will care for all your wants. Only, do not spend the night in the square." So he brought him into his house and gave the donkeys feed. And they washed their feet, and ate and drank.

As they were making their hearts merry, behold, the men of the city, worthless fellows, surrounded the house, beating on the door. And they said to the old man, the master of the house, "Bring out the man who came into your house, that we may know him." And the man, the master of the house, went out to them and said to them, "No, my brothers, do not act so wickedly; since this man has come into my house, do not do this vile thing. Behold, here are my virgin daughter and his concubine. Let me bring them out now. Violate them and do with them what seems good to you, but against this man do not do this outrageous thing." But the men would not listen to him. So the man seized his concubine and made her go out to them. And they knew her and abused her all night until the morning. And as the dawn began to break, they let her go. And as morning appeared, the woman came and fell down at the door of the man's house where her master was, until it was light.

And her master rose up in the morning, and when he opened the doors of the house and went out to go on his way, behold, there was his concubine lying at the door of the house, with her hands on the threshold. He said to her, "Get up, let us be going." But there was no answer. Then he put her on the donkey, and the man rose up and went away to his home. And when he entered his house, he took a knife, and taking hold of his concubine he divided her, limb by limb, into twelve pieces, and sent her throughout all the territory of Israel. And all who saw it said, "Such a thing has never happened or been seen from the day that the people of Israel came up out of the land of Egypt until this day; consider it, take counsel, and speak."

—JUDGES 19

OF ALL THE VILE, gruesome tales of horror from within the bleak recesses of human depravity, this story from Judges 19 ranks among the worst. At first blush, the narrative of the Levite and his concubine doesn't appear to teach anything. It only makes our stomachs churn and our faces sour in disgust. But the horror story of Judges 19 deserves a closer look. Here, the ghostly opera known as the Book of Judges reaches an X-rated crescendo. Most shockingly, the depravity of Judges 19 is not committed by some crazy sado-masochistic heathen cannibal rapists that escaped the ninth circle of hell. The most nausea-inducing story in the Bible has been brought to you compliments of God's people. These were supposed to be the good guys. These were the people who had the Ten Commandments. These were the covenant people of God, set apart to bless the nations. Now, I'm not suggesting that these psychos should be equated with your average friendly neighborhood Baptists. But these nut-jobs from the tribe of Benjamin make the men of Sodom look like a bunch of Sesame Street characters in comparison.

Let this sink in: The human heart, when left to its own devises, is radically corrupt and capable of great evil (Jer 17:9–10). When we stand outside the saving and sustaining grace of God, we sink into a swirling vortex of rot. The God-void is a horrible nightmare. In examining Judges 19, if we can see through the brutal rape, murder, and dismemberment, and somehow get past the sick, twisted, and demented debauchery, this story should remind the contemporary Christian church that one of its greatest threats might just be the depravity of its own members' hearts. This is not to say that Christians are worse people than others. To the contrary, I think Christ-followers who are redeemed by God's grace and indwelt by his Spirit can be made incrementally better through conformity to the image of Christ. We call this sanctification, the process of being made holy. But no Christian should ever fail to remember who and what they once were apart from Christ and what they might revert to apart from his grace. No one should think they're immune to the effects of utter moral filth. If anything, thank God you haven't fallen so low.

Judges 19 is about as low as it gets. Sanitized, inspirational books from the Christian living section of the local Bible bookstore do not contain beautifully illustrated devotional commentaries on the Judges 19. I've never seen an oil on canvas of "Dismembered Whore and Crazed Levite with Knife" on the walls of a church. Thankfully, no such painting exists.

Yet, this scar on the face of the history of God's chosen people does exist. It invites us to take a closer look. Judges 19 is a blaring wake-up call, reminding us that we are in desperate need of a faithful priest, a worthy king, and a true savior. God loves his people. Jesus gave his life for his unfaithful bride. He redeemed the wretched. He died for those who deserve death.

A ROTTEN PEOPLE

There's a lot going on in this story. Judges 19 revolves around a man from the priestly tribe of Levi, known simply as the Levite. That should be easy enough to remember. This particular Levite is a scoundrel-filled scum-sack with little human decency.

Next, we have the Levite's concubine, known as the concubine. Very original. However, as the narrative unfolds, she is sometimes referred to as his wife, or *issah*, sometimes referred to as a servant girl, or *naarah*, and other times referred to as a concubine, or *pileges*. The context implies the term concubine is most fitting. She was purchased, perhaps from a poor family, and most likely used by the Levite for sexual gratification.[1]

1. Patai, *Sex and Marriage in the Bible*, 41.

Slightly less important to the story are a host of secondary characters, including the girl's father, the Levite's male servant, and the old man from Gibeah and his virgin daughter. Finally, we have a host of rapists—a mob of perverted reprobates. A couple of donkeys also show up in the story, but I don't think they play much of a role beyond transporting the Levite's collection of fine cabernets and merlots.

Here's the gist of the story: After being treated like a whore by the Levite, it seems the girl ran away and played the whore with some other man, before returning to her father's home. Her father likely felt embarrassed that the daughter he sold had left her "husband" and returned home. Hence, his unusually gracious hospitality to the Levite who came searching for the runaway concubine, albeit four months later. It seems the father was trying to patch things up. So far, nothing seems too out of the ordinary in this particular chapter of human depravity. The story takes an unusual turn, however, when the Levite and his concubine decided to leave the in-laws house and head back to the Levite's hometown. Along the way, they stopped on the wrong side of the tracks, in the wrong town, at the wrong time of day. It was late, so they tried to get a room at the local motel. Unfortunately, there was no vacancy at the Lovers Lane Inn—you know, the one with the heart shaped hot tub and the vibrating bed. So, they decided to sleep under the stars in the city park. Fortunately, a nice old-timer saw them on a park bench and invited them in to spend the night.

As they were minding their own business, enjoying microwave dinners from the local gas station, and watching *Wheel of Fortune*, they heard a knock at the door. It was a group of evil men from around town. In true *Deliverance*-style (as banjo music played in the background), the aforementioned evil men demanded they deliver the Levite for their sexual gratification. The old man tried to offer his own virgin daughter, but the Levite insisted on sending his concubine. To deter the onslaught and save himself, the Levite tossed the young woman outside and let the men abuse her throughout the night. Around dawn they dumped her body on the front lawn and she crawled to the door, only half-conscious. But in his great compassion, the Levite stayed in bed and caught a few more winks. Later, as the sun came up, he finally opened the door, and seeing her ravished beaten body, callously told her to get her lazy carcass up and make him some breakfast. She didn't respond, so he threw her in the back of his truck (or on the back of the donkey) and drove the rest of the way home.

At this point, the Levite had to do some serious thinking. What to do with the body? After pacing the room and downing a couple of six-packs, he was struck with the brilliant idea to take his former lover, cut her into twelve pieces, and FedEx her all over Israel. What better way to honor your concubine and former lover, whose death you were responsible for? The whole thing is sickening.

It is impossible to read this story and feel nothing for this poor girl, though we know little about her. We might ask: Was her heart truly set on evil when she ran away to play the whore? What led her to run away? Was she simply the victim of an abusive lover and an oppressive society? Was the Levite's treatment of her justified in his own depraved mind, and motivated by his jealousy? Drama always bleeds in between the lines, and speculation may allow a conjectured glimpse into the complex humanity of the characters. There are doubtless many details we simply don't know. Regardless, the essential facts are communicated in shaking detail.

It's on these facts that the theological weight of the story hinges. Here's what we know: God's people fell into a level of depravity as bad or worse than anything conjured by the wicked Canaanites whom God had commanded the Israelites to drive from the land.

This story may have reminded you of an analogous Bible story we covered previously. Commentator, Dale Ralph Davis, notes the similarity and deliberateness between this story and that of Genesis 19, where the men of Sodom form a mob and seek to abuse and rape two angels.[2] This clear reference to Genesis, he thinks, was an intentional way of accusing the people of God.[3] If you think the men of the heathen city of Sodom are bad, wait until you see what God's own covenant people are capable of. Tim Keller's remarks on the subject are worth quoting at length:

> Sodom is the great Old Testament example of rebellion against God that rightly brings upon itself the judgment of God. The parallel between that pagan city and Israelite Gibeah carries an obvious message. Here are the people of God, who have been given the covenants of Abraham and Moses, the law and the prophets, the tabernacle, the exodus, and more recently the savior-judges. Yet despite all this, they are no better than the Canaanites and pagan

2. Davis, *Judges*, 209.
3. Ibid.

nations who had received none of these blessings. God's people prove to be no better.[4]

Who is to save them from such wretchedness and concupiscence? In this case, no judge is sent. No wise king exacts vengeance for these heinous crimes. No God-ordained savior appears in glory to heal the land of this evil. Israel will suffer for its corruption.

A REDEEMED PEOPLE

In Judges 1, things are bad. In Judges 19, things are worse. The cycle of sin, oppression, repentance, and deliverance is ironically followed by more of the same. None of the judges sent by God could permanently heal the land. None of Israel's saviors could permanently save. No generation of sinners is better than the previous generation, and no human savior is more capable than the one before. Broken people can't fix broken people. In spite of every human attempt to get it right, it's always wrong. The harder you try to fix it, the worse it gets. It's like watching the Three Stooges try to repair a minor leak in a small pipe. Sure, they succeed in patching the hole *and* in bringing down the whole house while they're at it. That's us. Beware not to sneer at the Levite and the rapists of Gibeah. Under the right circumstances, you might do worse.

Judges 19 teaches us that sinners need Jesus. Fools need Jesus. Insecure people need Jesus. Heartbroken people need Jesus. Depraved and confused people need Jesus. People who are struggling with their identity and self-worth need Jesus. People who are trying desperately to fix themselves need Jesus—the only one who can fix us. We need Jesus to impute his righteousness to us and heal our heart with his overwhelming love. But we also need Jesus to sanctify our hearts and purify us as we walk in repentance.

The church is comprised of sick people who have been, and are being, healed. The church is made up of redeemed scoundrels. Look for yourself on this list provided by the apostle Paul in 1 Corinthians 6:9–11:

> Or do you not know that the unrighteous will not inherit the kingdom of God? Do not be deceived: neither the sexually immoral, nor idolaters, nor adulterers, nor men who practice homosexuality, nor thieves, nor the greedy, nor drunkards, nor revilers, nor swindlers will inherit the kingdom of God. And such were some of

4. Keller, *Judges for You*, 185.

you. But you were washed, you were sanctified, you were justified
in the name of the Lord Jesus Christ and by the Spirit of our God.

I think that covers everyone. It's what we were and what we might revert to
apart from the grace of the Father who sent his Son to pay the penalty we
deserve. Apart from Christ we all stand condemned. We stand among the
men of Sodom and Gibeah. We stand in shame beside the heartless Levite.
We stand with the concubine in her fear and pain. But praise be to God for
the saving love he extended to this world in all its horror. New Testament
scholar, D.A. Carson, aptly notes: "God's love in sending the Lord Jesus is
to be admired not because it is extended to so big a thing as the world, but
to so bad a thing; not to so many people, as to such wicked people."[5] To
think that Jesus died for the savages of Judges 19. To think that Jesus died
for you and me.

STUDY QUESTIONS

1. Judges 19 focuses on the sin for God's own people. What do you
   think are the biggest sins among God's people (the church) today?

2. Read Judges 19 and identify all the characters in the story. Are any of
   them morally upright? Explain.

3. Why do you suppose the Levite waits so long (four months) before
   seeking out his runaway concubine? Why do you suppose the concubine's father is so eager to welcome the Levite?

4. Read Numbers 3:5–10. Who were the Levites in the Bible? What was
   their role? Does the Levite in this story walk in a manner worthy of
   his office?

5. Carson, *Difficult Doctrine of the Love of God*, 17.

5. Compare the account of Judges 19 with that of Genesis 19. What are some similarities and differences? Are the men of Israel better than those of Sodom? What makes the Israelites worse?

6. Are there sins in your life (and in the church as a whole) that are being ignored?

7. In what ways is Jesus able to repair human sin, depravity, shame, and brokenness? See John 10:10, Luke 4:16–21, Luke 19:9–10, and Acts 4:11–12.

The New Testament

11

Eaten by Worms — Acts 12

Now Herod was angry with the people of Tyre and Sidon, and they came to him with one accord, and having persuaded Blastus, the king's chamberlain, they asked for peace, because their country depended on the king's country for food. On an appointed day Herod put on his royal robes, took his seat upon the throne, and delivered an oration to them. And the people were shouting, "The voice of a god, and not of a man!" Immediately an angel of the Lord struck him down, because he did not give God the glory, and he was eaten by worms and breathed his last. But the word of God increased and multiplied.

—Acts 12:20–24

WE ARE BORN INTO a world of decay. The human body eventually breaks down and succumbs to the ultimate atrophy of death. Most people don't want to think about this. Once in the grave, supposing we haven't been cremated, our body will decompose. Soon after death, various micro-organisms living in the body begin to feed on tissue, causing bloating and the release of gases. Putrid liquids and foul stenches then seep from the body. The putrescent cadaver attracts flies, who lay their eggs in the rotting flesh—a gourmet feast for the new brood of young maggots. Eventually, advanced decay leaves us with nothing but a dry skeleton.

It's gross. But it's the way things are. We wouldn't expect the order of decomposition to be any different. So, if the process were reversed in some way, we would take note. Suppose the maggots showed up prior to death. Suppose the maggots ate you from the inside out while you were still alive. Suppose your soul was so rotten—your spirit so dead—you putrefied even as you went on living. It sounds like a scene from the mind of a horror novelist. But for one unfortunate Bible character, this was all too real.

Herod Agrippa, the puppet king of Galilee, an insignificant corner of the Roman Empire, elevated himself to the place of God and learned that true gods don't die slow painful deaths. True gods don't succumb to worm infestations. True gods are worthy of worship, not judgment. We read in Acts 12 that Herod Agrippa was an arrogant fool—a thug-filled scoundrel-coated lowlife served with a side of spicy miscreant salad and garnished with a pinch of jerkweed. Like today's insecure celebrities with too much media attention, Herod's ego swelled. He elevated himself to the place of God. This was a mistake. God reminded him there can only be one Lord of the universe.

The story of Herod Agrippa is more than a story about being eaten alive by flesh-devouring maggots. It's more than a gruesome tale of death, gore, and heavenly messengers of death. At its core, it's a story of idolatry, but not the gold, silver, or stone variety. This idolatry took the form of self-worship. Public figures aren't the only ones susceptible to the temptation toward self-worship as the flattering voices of admirers call out: "The voice of a god." We all worship something, whether we know it or not. We worship the image looking back at us in the mirror. Even for those of us who don't have admirers, we create the illusion that we do. We easily become our own false gods. Some of us learn this the hard way. Herod did.

MISPLACED WORSHIP

The name Herod will likely evoke feelings of disdain. Thuggery was an important part of the family legacy of Herod Agrippa's predecessors. His grandfather, Herod the Great, is the one we read about in the Christmas narrative who put to death all the baby boys in Bethlehem in an attempt to locate and murder the infant Jesus (Matt 2:16). Herod the Great apparently hated Christmas, ugly Christmas sweaters, sugar cookies, and peppermint mochas. Under his reign, no one was allowed to listen to Mariah Carrey's *All I Want for Christmas is You*. He was a real jerk. Next there was Herod Agrippa's uncle, Herod Antipas, who beheaded John the Baptist (Matt 14:1–12; Mark 6:14–29; Luke 9:7–9) and who oversaw the trial of Jesus

(Luke 23:7–12).[1] This particular Herod also enjoyed belly dancers, adultery, and birthday parties with cupcakes and pinatas.

Finally, we come to Herod Agrippa, who also wanted to be remembered as an insalubrious character of questionable moral judgment.[2] The opening of Acts 12 tells us that Herod beheaded the apostle James and imprisoned the apostle Peter with the intent of bringing him to trial, and eventually death. Luckily for Peter, an angel showed up and busted him out of prison using angel power, a metal file, and a rock hammer. But anyway, Herod Agrippa was a persecutor of the church, whose life later became characterized by vanity and self-absorption. By the time we get to the worm episode, Herod Agrippa had established himself as a true butthead of biblical proportions.

We read in Acts 12:20 that Herod had been disputing with the authorities of the Phoenician cities of Tyre and Sidon, which were coastal municipalities located in modern day Lebanon. Though we don't know all the details of the dispute, we do know that Herod had the upper hand in the argument and that the people were prepared to listen to his terms because he controlled all the shipments of Doritos and Cosmic Brownies into Phoenicia.

After arriving in Phoenicia in his private jet, he was escorted into a lavish conference center where he stepped up onto the platform and began his speech: "Hey folks, it's good to be here today . . . but at my age, it's good to be anywhere!" A wave of chuckles swept through the crowd. "Now, really folks, I want what's best for you . . . ." He then went on to convince the people that he was on their side and that the tariffs were in their best interest. He was an average Joe—a good ol' hardworking guy just like them. By the time he finished his speech with a heartwarming story about a boy and a lost puppy, he had won them over.

It also helped that Herod wore designer clothing. He owned several Armani suits. Acts 12:21 tells us that Herod wore a kingly robe that seems to have communicated the self-righteous pride that often comes with the office he held. The Jewish historian Josephus, in his *Antiquities*, speaks of Herod's robe as an elaborate garment woven of silver thread that when

---

1. For more on Herod Antipas see, Jensen, "Antipas" 42–6.

2. Herod Agrippa I, whom we meet in Acts 12, is not to be confused with Herod Agrippa II, whom we encounter in Acts 25–26, and who actually appears somewhat sympathetic toward the apostle Paul.

reflecting the light of the sun, dazzled all onlookers.[3] He came before them to impress and amaze. His heart was ready to welcome any admiration he could get.

The combination of Herod's pompous attitude and the flattery of the people did not end well for him. His prideful self-worship led to his downfall. This kind of self-worship happens when we give into the temptation to think ourselves better than we are—to exalt ourselves above our allotted position or to think of ourselves a little too often. It's no different than the "me-culture" we live in today. Maybe Herod was born in the wrong century. He would have loved Twitter, or X, or whatever it's called these days. He would have loved Instagram. In the twenty-first century, everyone's an influencer; everyone's a model. Photoshop, image-editing software, the right camera-angle, and good lighting can transform the most hideous wildebeest into an absolute smoke show. The internet can make anyone look good. It can help anyone flaunt a false image where we hide our worst features and qualities, and accent only what we want people to see. We do it all the time. We do it at school; we do it at work; we do it at church. Herod worshipped himself and wanted others to do the same. Maybe we can all relate a little.

As the crowd shouted praise to Herod, he basked in the glory. Praise that belongs to God alone, was hijacked by Herod in his pride. Because of this self-worship, an angel struck him with miniature versions of those hideous worms from *Dune*. The worms burrowed through his internal organs and ate him alive. Here, we must pause to appreciate the violence of this particular death. The order in which the events unfolded is significant. Some might suppose that for Herod the dying part comes before the worm infestation part. After all, that's normally how things work. But I'm not sure that's how the grammar plays out in the original Greek. The most natural reading of Acts 12:23 seems to align well with the idea that worms ate him, which *then* led to him breathing his last.

The moral of the story is that self-worship is self-destructive. Herod Agrippa is not remembered for his handsome features, his alluring attire, or his eloquent discourses—he's the guy who was eaten by worms. Whenever we worship anything other than God, we are destroyed from within. Misdirected worship eats away our soul. Misplaced worship is cannibalization of the soul. It's like the unfortunate space mobster, Pizza the Hut, in *Spaceballs*. He was made of pizza. And when he became locked in his limo,

---

3. Josephus, *Antiquities of the Jews*, chapter 19.

unable to escape, he ended up eating himself to death. He was delicious. He couldn't get enough of himself. Now, for those who are unable to appreciate the sophisticated humor and general refinement of *Spaceballs*, you may relate better to the myth of Narcissus, the Greek god who fell in love with his own reflection in a pool of water, and unable to turn his gaze away, pined away, and died. Self-worship is self-defeating, self-destroying, and self-stultifying.

TRUE WORSHIP

How can we ensure that self-confidence and healthy self-esteem don't transmute into unhealthy self-focus and self-worship? I think our proximity to God helps us identify an answer. When we stand in the overwhelming luminescence of God's glory, we begin to see ourselves for what we are—not worthless beings, but beings humbled by God's grace even as we are elevated by his love for us. God created us with dignity and crowned us with honor (Ps 8:3–8). In Acts 14, the apostles Paul and Barnabas were given an opportunity to walk into the same sin as Herod. They chose to glorify God, instead. We read that after Paul and Barnabas miraculously healed a crippled man in the city of Lystra, the people attempted to worship them as gods. Does this sound familiar? But unlike Herod, the reaction of Paul and Barnabas was to tear their robes in grief and agony over the blasphemy of the people, and to plead with their would-be worshippers to repent and believe the one true God—the only one truly capable of miracles. This is a radical contrast to the reaction of Herod, who gladly accepted the worship of men, blinding himself to his own fallen spiritual condition and his need for God.

We live in a society that's saturated with self-worship. But the good news of Acts 12 is found on verse 24: "But the word of God increased and multiplied." The word of God has an impact far beyond the impact of any word of man. The transformative power of the gospel has a greater and more significant effect than any gospel of self. God can redirect those who are self-focused through his powerful life-changing word.

Herod died, but the word of God increased and multiplied. Self-worship destroyed lives, but the word of God increased and multiplied. Pride makes us fools, but the word of God can increase and multiply in us, giving us wisdom in our application of knowledge of the truth. And how does this happen? It happens when we draw near to God in worship. God initiates worship by virtue of being worthy of worship. As we receive his mercy, grace, and love, our natural response can be none other than worship. As God's word becomes more central, more influential, more directive, and more abundant, we will be inclined to pour out worship toward him.

The heart of the gospel is not to try harder at fixing our self-absorption and pride. Instead, the Bible tells us to allow God's word to increase and multiply in our lives. It invites us to ask ourselves: Where is my god and who is my god? What brings me joy in life? Do I take ultimate pleasure in my own abilities, my own talents, my capacities, my productivity, my achievements, and my appearance? Are my words and actions formulated with the intent to receive glory for myself? Do I seek the approval of others for self-validation? Am I preoccupied with all that I offer this world, while forgetting all that God has done for me?

If we don't let God's word spread over us, and saturate our lives, and humble our hearts, and transform our souls, we can never know what true worship is. True worship abounds when we acknowledge that we cannot save ourselves. True worship can only take place when we humbly bow before the thrice-holy God of the universe, confess our inadequacy, and acknowledge that Christ alone is worthy of praise because he gave his life for us on the cross.

True worship—God-centered, gospel-motivated worship—is devoid of pride and egoism. It recognizes that God is the sole focus of our adoration, and that Jesus is the only savior. True worship invites God's word to increase and multiply in our lives so that we may think a little less of ourselves and a lot more of God. True worship affirms with John the Baptist: "I must decrease, he must increase" (John 3:30). So, as we reflect on the life and death of Herod Agrippa, let us stand with the apostle Paul in counting all our achievements, possession, status, influence, and connections as rubbish for the sake of knowing Christ (Phil. 3:8). Let us be true worshippers, and let us preach the gospel to ourselves daily, living out the gospel so that others will become true worshippers as well.

STUDY QUESTIONS

1. Have you ever experienced fame, even on a small scale? How did it change your view of yourself?

2. Read Acts 12. How does Herod treat the apostles? What seems to be his motivation in persecuting the church? What does this tell us about the kind of person he was?

3. Herod seems to have been easily influenced by the approval of others. How has the approval of others influenced you for good or for bad?

4. What does Acts 12 teach us about the character of God?

5. Why do you suppose God allowed James to perish though he allowed Peter to survive?

6. Both Peter (v. 7) and Herod (v. 23) were "struck," or touched by an angel of the Lord. How do these two incidences compare and contrast?

7. What were Herod's sins in this passage? What do you think was the sin beneath the sin (the deeper issue in Herod's heart) that led to his judgment by God?

8. At the end of Acts 12 we read: "But the word of God increased and multiplied." See also, Isaiah 55:11 and Hebrews 4:12. What is the "word of God," and why is it important? Explain why the message of salvation in Christ is able to overcome the powers of this world.

12

Slain by the Spirit — Acts 5

But a man named Ananias, with his wife Sapphira, sold a piece of property, and with his wife's knowledge he kept back for himself some of the proceeds and brought only a part of it and laid it at the apostles' feet. But Peter said, "Ananias, why has Satan filled your heart to lie to the Holy Spirit and to keep back for yourself part of the proceeds of the land? While it remained unsold, did it not remain your own? And after it was sold, was it not at your disposal? Why is it that you have contrived this deed in your heart? You have not lied to man but to God." When Ananias heard these words, he fell down and breathed his last. And great fear came upon all who heard of it. The young men rose and wrapped him up and carried him out and buried him. After an interval of about three hours his wife came in, not knowing what had happened. And Peter said to her, "Tell me whether you sold the land for so much." And she said, "Yes, for so much." But Peter said to her, "How is it that you have agreed together to test the Spirit of the Lord? Behold, the feet of those who have buried your husband are at the door, and they will carry you out." Immediately she fell down at his feet and breathed her last. When the young men came in they found her dead, and they carried her out and buried her beside her husband. And great fear came upon the whole church and upon all who heard of these things.

—Acts 5:1–11

GIVING TO THE CHURCH has long been a sensitive matter. Christians sometimes speak of the importance of *tithing*, or giving a tenth.[1] A tenth can feel like a lot, especially when we have bills to pay and mouths to feed. But we're supposed to give, and we're supposed to do it willingly and generously. God loves a cheerful giver, as they say (2 Cor 9:7). Cheerful or not, most churches I know will take any giver. The electric bill doesn't pay itself. Some Christians are adamant that tithing is a mandate that should be obeyed. It's a privilege and an exercise in faith. Others will quickly retort that to mandate tithing is to usurp grace and lay an unnecessary guilt trip on people who can't or don't feel called to give. The cynic in me suspects that this latter position is more about people not wanting to drop their hard-earned money in the collection plate. Let's be honest here. Sometimes we just don't want to give. Without a robust biblical theology of giving, we can easily make excuses. I have.

But then there's the other big tithing conundrum: Should the tithe be calculated on the basis of gross or net income? Hmm. Interesting question. Should it be calculated on the income before we've paid our bills, or income that's left after we've paid our bills? Again, I suspect these kinds of questions might arise as another pseudo-pious attempt to look like we care about getting it right, while in actuality, we're just looking for an excuse to hold back a little on giving. By the way, I'm not planning on offering any insights on this matter, because 1) this chapter is about a lot more than just tithing, and 2) I'd rather make some space here to poke fun at the Medieval church for a moment.

You see, when it came to tithing, the Medieval Roman Catholic potentates got themself into some trouble. It's not cheap to build extravagant and ostentatious monuments to the greatness of the church. Sixteenth century tithes and offerings simply weren't getting the job done. At first, the Pope and his buddies tried to raise money by hosting a car-wash fundraiser in the Vatican parking lot. But they ran into a setback. Nuns in full habits washing cars simply didn't draw the crowd the church had hoped for. Moreover, multiple failed bake sales in front of the local Walmart didn't help either. I have it on good authority that banana bread was not popular among Medieval European peasants.

One day, while the Pope was soaking in his bubble bath, he had the brilliant idea of selling get-out-of-hell cards, called *indulgences*. Immediately

---

1. See Leviticus 27:30–34. Other Scriptures like Genesis 14:17–24 also refer to tithing that is disassociated from the law.

he summoned his loyal inquisitor, Johann Tetzel, to carry out the new and exciting fundraiser. Roughly, an indulgence, of the kind we're concerned with here, was a payment made to the church that would reduce the time the payer's dead loved ones would spend in purgatory burning off their sins before being allowed to walk through the pearly gates. Put crudely, ten dollars might take ten years off a person's suffering. Tradition states the Pope's talented and notorious peddler of indulgences, Tetzel, coined the well-known refrain: "As soon as the coin in the coffer rings, the soul from purgatory springs."[2]

Some Protestants have their own version of indulgences. We call it the *prosperity gospel*. The basic premise is to give as much as possible to the church so that God will bless you with a bigger house and more cool stuff. The more you give the more you get. Meanwhile, as you are waiting for the big payoff to come in, the pastor and beneficiary of your generosity is purchasing a yacht, lavish homes, sports cars, private jets, and plastic surgery. A simple cost-benefit analysis reveals that this isn't a good deal for you. The preacher gets richer, you get poorer. But at least you get to feel good for having financed the pastor's wife's mink coat. That's the Protestant version of indulgences in a nutshell.

Now, why am I talking about all this? Because early on in the history of the church, a botched attempt at generosity got some people killed. At the end of Acts 4, some guy named Barnabas sold a field and gave all the proceeds to the apostles to assuage the needs of the impoverished. He became an instant rock star. Everyone applauded and told him what a great Christian he was. Then, like a bunch of *Top Gun* pilots, they gave him a cool call sign: "Son of Encouragement," which he had tattooed on his arm, or something like that (Acts 4:36). When Ananias and his wife Sapphira saw this, they decided they would also like some accolades and cool nicknames like, for example, Goose and Maverick. So, they sold a field, kept some of the money for themselves, and then told everyone they gave all the money to the apostles, even though they hadn't. Because of their lie, the Holy Spirit showed up to kick gluteus maximus and take names.

It turns out the real issue was not about giving, but lying. Ananias and his wife gave their offering with false motives for the praise of humans rather than for the glory of God. This was a bad idea.

---

2. For more on the events surrounding the sale of indulgences and the history of the Protestant Reformation see, Bainton, *Here I Stand*.

DO NOT GRIEVE THE HOLY SPIRIT OF GOD

Ananias and Sapphira lied to the Holy Spirit. They wanted attention for their good deeds, much like the hypocrites Jesus addresses in the Sermon on the Mount—the ones who pray into megaphones on the street corners and post selfies on social media so everyone knows how great they are (Matt 6:5). Ananias and his wife wanted the clatter of their gold to resonate from the offering plate like the clash of an oversized Chinese gong. They wanted to be seen and heard.

Twice, we are told that their heart was in the wrong place. They had contrived deception in their *heart* (Acts 5:4). Satan had filled their *heart* (Acts 5:3). The heart, or *kardia* from the original Greek, usually refers to something akin to the inner being, the reason, the bowels of passion and thought, or the inner most disposition of the self. More than the anatomic seat of the emotions, the heart represents the very core of the person. It refers to our reason, our mind, our center of virtue, and our inner individuality. The heart represents what is truly at the center of a person. A heart of deception, filled by Satan, is a heart that lacks true conversion. It's a disordered and disoriented heart. Now, bear in mind, we aren't told that Ananias and Sapphira are false believers. Instead, we see a couple who are publicly professing faith in Christ while living more like heathens. They had deceived themselves while attempting to deceive the Holy Spirit of God.

It was a seller's market, so Ananias posted his five-acre lakeside lot on Zillow and waited to see what would happen. Sure enough, it sold. Now he could buy that new RV he'd been wanting. There would even be a little left over. He took the leftovers, made a wire transfer to the local church, then got up and made a speech about how God had led him to sell some of his real estate and sacrificially give an extravagant gift to the church. All the while, his wife shouted: "Amen! Hallelujah! Preach it!"

That Sunday, they walked out of the church as heroes in the eyes of their peers. What they didn't expect when they got home was the apostle Peter sitting at their kitchen table helping himself to leftover tuna noodle casserole and drinking their craft IPA from a wine glass. Peter wiped the froth from his lips, belched discretely, and spoke in an authoritative apostolic voice: "I don't give a rat's derriere (sorry, this is a Christian PG-rated book) about the money, but seriously, did you have to lie to the Holy Spirit? Bad move. Since you're a liar and an idiot, the Holy Spirit is going to perform a Dark Vadar-style windpipe pinch on you." Immediately, Ananias fell over dead.

Moments later, Sapphira walked in as Peter was polishing off his second piece of carrot cake. As she was about to ask him what the hell he was doing in her pantry, he interrogated her as well. Like a parent giving their child one more chance to tell the truth before grounding them for a month, Peter asked: "Is there anything else you need to tell me about the sale of the land?" Sapphira responded, "Of course not! What's your problem? And why are you sitting in my kitchen? And why are eating my food? And where is Ananias?"

At this, Peter stood before Sapphira like Gandolf rebuking Bilbo, and speaking in the black tongue of Mordor, called down a curse on Sapphira, who keeled over and went "gentle into that good night." Moral of the story: Don't mess with Peter when he's ornery after a long Sunday morning church service. Also, don't lie to the Holy Spirit, especially when he has only just come to indwell his church and fill them with wisdom, power, and strength to carry out the mission of Jesus with courage and love (Acts 2; John 14:15–31).

An important parallel exists between this account and that of Leviticus 10:1–3. Aaron's sons were consumed by holy fire because of their illicit sacrifice. This took place immediately after the revelation of God's law. I suspect that on some level, they were judged harshly to set a precedent for the people—take God's newly revealed law seriously. Their sin was used to make an example that would be remembered for generations. In a similar way, Ananias and Sapphira became an object lesson for the newly formed church. God's gracious provision of life through the gospel is not something to be taken lightly. The promised Holy Spirit had shown up in a powerful way, and now these clowns were testing him like they were in charge.

Hypocrisy is not just about saying one thing and doing another. It's also about trying to lie to God while pretending God doesn't see us in our double life.

KEEP IN STEP WITH THE SPIRIT

Though most Christians probably wouldn't say it, we sometimes act like the Holy Spirit is just some mindless force we can use at our convenience. We bark orders at him, commanding him like a genie to give us what we want. We treat the Spirit—the almighty God of the universe—like a magic power. We think we can hide the truth of our innermost sins and self-deceit from the very Spirit who indwells us. Ananias and Sapphira lied to the Spirit in lying to themselves. And they lied to the Spirit in lying to the church.

We are of the same ilk as our unfortunate aforementioned forebearers. We try to self-justify our lies. I can only imagine the dialogue Ananias had in his head: "I gave every penny! I swear! I mean, I didn't give *all* the money, but I did give some of the money. I gave every penny of every dollar I gave. So, yeah, I gave every penny! I'm really a good and godly person. I think the church should appreciate the sacrifice I made. I did it for God. Sure, I love the accolades, but really, I gave every penny for God and to God. I hope God appreciates the sacrifice I've made."

And so the lie goes. It works out the same for every sin in our lives. If we have any self-awareness whatsoever, we probably see through ourselves. Those closest to us often see through us. God definitely sees through us. What base and vulgar ignorance would possess us to think God doesn't see our lie? Before we're tempted to treat the Holy Spirit with contempt or deceit, remember that the Spirit is our God. He's no joke.

The Holy Spirit, who raised Jesus from the dead, has the power to give us life (Rom 8:11). The Holy Spirit, who judged Ananias and Sapphira, has the power to take life. Our relationship with the Spirit should be reverential, among other things. The Spirit instructs us (John 14:26), empowers us (Acts 1:8), frees us of sin (Rom 8:2), preserves us for the day of final redemption (Eph 1:13–4), and reminds us of the truth (John 14:26). In John 14, the Spirit is referred to as our *paraclete*, or Comforter. But comforter from what? As Francis Chan aptly points out: Our need for a comforter presupposes the reality of some discomfort in our lives.[3] We all need comfort. And comfort refers to more than just a hug when we're feeling down. It seems Ananias and Sapphira needed the comfort of the Spirit to help them trust, to help walk in obedience to God in the safety and care of the Lord, and to comfort the church as they gave sacrificially to those in need. But rather than take comfort in the Comforter, they walked according to their fear—fear of looking bad in the eyes of the church, fear of not having enough for themselves, fear of humans rather than healthy reverence for God.

The Holy Spirit is the divine curator of our spirits. When he indwells us, our own spirit must submit to him. And when we resist the Spirit who seals us in God's promise for the day of redemption, we have resisted the Christ who gave his life for redemption, and the Father who adopted us

3. Chan, *Forgotten God*, 107.

into that redemption (Eph 1:3–14). God knows the thoughts of our heart. He knows our inner being—our mind, our spirit. Being truthful before God requires more than being honest with ourselves and those around us. Truthfulness seems to demand that we see God seeing us—that we make eye-contact, in a way. Truthfulness is to stand before God as he sees our sin and sees Christ's righteousness in us. We call this transparency. Only there are we able to embrace our proximity to God in the Spirit and worship him uninhibited.

STUDY QUESTIONS

1. When have you been caught in a lie? What happened?

2. Reflect on Acts 5:1–11. Who are Ananias and Sapphira? What did they do to offend God? How did the Holy Spirit of God respond to their sin?

3. Do you think God is too harsh in this situation? Compare with Leviticus 10:1–3. In both passages God is establishing something new among his people. How might these judgments serve as an example to the people?

4. Reflect on the idea that "great fear" came upon the people because of God's judgment. Was this a good thing for the church?

5. In what ways have you lied to the Spirit? In what ways might this passage be helpful in correcting our tendencies to treat the Holy Spirit like a mere "power" we can tap into and control as we see fit?

6. What does it mean to live honestly, or truthfully, before God?

7. How can you get better at honoring the Spirit in your worship of God? See Galatians 5:16–26 and Ephesians 4:30.

B

Grisly Suicide — Matthew 27 and Acts 1

Then when Judas, his betrayer, saw that Jesus was condemned, he changed his mind and brought back the thirty pieces of silver to the chief priests and the elders, saying, "I have sinned by betraying innocent blood." They said, "What is that to us? See to it yourself." And throwing down the pieces of silver into the temple, he departed, and he went and hanged himself. But the chief priests, taking the pieces of silver, said, "It is not lawful to put them into the treasury, since it is blood money." So they took counsel and bought with them the potter's field as a burial place for strangers. Therefore that field has been called the Field of Blood to this day. Then was fulfilled what had been spoken by the prophet Jeremiah, saying, "And they took the thirty pieces of silver, the price of him on whom a price had been set by some of the sons of Israel, and they gave them for the potter's field, as the Lord directed me."

—MATTHEW 27:3–10

In those days Peter stood up among the brothers (the company of persons was in all about 120) and said, "Brothers, the Scripture had to be fulfilled, which the Holy Spirit spoke beforehand by the mouth of David concerning Judas, who became a guide to those who arrested Jesus. For he was numbered among us and was allotted his share in this ministry." (Now this man acquired a field with the reward of his wickedness, and falling headlong he burst open in the middle *and all his bowels gushed out. And it became known to all the inhabitants of Jerusalem, so that the field was called in their own language Akeldama, that is, Field of Blood.)*

—ACTS 1:15–19

BETRAYAL STINGS. IT'S A particularly painful offense because, by definition, it always comes from someone close to you. We expect our enemies to hate us. We don't expect our friends to stab us in the back. We certainly don't expect them to turn us over to an outraged mob who will beat us, mock us, and crucify us. The moment Judas betrayed Jesus he became a household name. His infamous treachery cemented his name in history and pop culture. The new wave British metal band, Judas Priest, clearly paid him homage. Lady Gaga's song *Judas* seems to have done the same. Other bands like Petra and Metallica produced songs referencing Judas' kiss—a kiss that symbolized a devious and treacherous greeting, and that indicated which man the soldiers would seize in the obscurity of night (Matt 26:48–9; Mark 14:44–5; Luke 22:47–8). Judas is remembered for all the wrong reasons. His name is synonymous with *betrayer*.

There are probably better ways to get cool bands named after you than being a perfidious jerk and initiating the death of the savior of the world. What good is it for a man to gain thirty pieces of silver but lose his soul (Matt 16:26)? The night he was betrayed, Jesus mournfully pronounced woe to the one by whom the Son of Man would be betrayed: "It would have been better for that man if he had not been born" (Matt 26:24). I suspect that means things aren't going well for Judas in the afterlife. Dante, in his *Inferno*, actually has Judas hanging out with Satan in the ninth circle of hell, where betrayers are forced to listen to Kenny G music on repeat, while waiting in line at the DMV for eternity. Dante's imagery of Judas' demise is fanciful. He takes some significant liberties in interpreting Jesus' "woe" against Judas. Poor Judas finds himself dangling from the mouth of one of Satan's three ugly faces, his head being chewed while the devil's claws repeatedly skin his back.[1]

Having never visited hell, I can't tell you how accurate Dante is in his description. But I will tell you this: The biblical description of hell's eternal fire doesn't sound nice either (Matt 25:41). While we can only speculate

1. Dante, *Divine Comedy: Inferno*, 34.58–63.

about the details of Judas' current situation, we need not speculate about how he ended up there. Scripture tells us that shortly after handing Jesus over to the authorities, Judas was filled with regret about the betrayal, at which point he went out and hanged himself (Matt 27:5). No wait, that can't be it. Doesn't it also say he went out into a field and fell forward so that his body burst open, and his intestines spilled out (Acts 1:18)? So, which account is it then?

As with many other putative discrepancies in Scripture, skeptics and assorted antagonists to the Bible like to point out that the Scriptures can't be divinely inspired if God can't even get his own story straight. Matthew and Luke (the author of Acts) should have consulted one another on the details before attempting to write contradictory stories, or so the argument goes. Apparent discrepancies and contradictions in Scripture shouldn't be glibly dismissed or ignored. Difficulties in Scripture should be acknowledged and humbly investigated. The way ancient authors practiced their craft differs from how we write today. Ancient writers conflated, streamlined, embellished, reworded, reordered, and abridged in ways that wouldn't be acceptable today. That doesn't mean they didn't speak the truth. It doesn't mean their accounts are uninspired and irreconcilable.

Though I understand the anxiety we might experience in comparing the two accounts of Judas, I think it's misplaced. My suggestion: Both accounts are true. While Matthew is explaining the way Judas died, Luke is describing the final condition of Judas' body. It isn't difficult to imagine that Judas hanged himself, after which point his body began to swell and bloat in the hot Judean sun. Bodies don't burst open without significant decomposition. Eventually the tree branch broke, and Judas fell to the ground like an overfilled water balloon. Commentator Joseph Smith (the 21st century Christian author, *not* the nineteenth century founder of Mormonism), suggests that "this explanation is all the more likely because the Greek phrase 'falling headlong' can also mean 'swelling up,' creating a picture of decomposition and disembowelment that is truly disgusting."[2]

Matthew wants to focus on Judas as a morbid lifeless pinata swinging gently from a branch. Luke wants to focus on the maggot-infested pile of gore that was left on the ground. Why? Commentator, James Bejon, has an interesting take on the emphases of these two accounts. He suggests that Matthew and Luke might be drawing parallels between Judas and several Old Testament figures. In Matthew's account, Bejon reasons that

2. Smith, *Sex and Violence in the Bible*, 135.

Jesus parallels David, where Judas parallels Absolom, the son of David, who betrayed him and attempted to usurp him as king (2 Sam 15–18). If David was betrayed by Absolom, who died a hanged man, so too Jesus is the Davidic king betrayed by Judas, who met the same fate. Bejon has it that "If Jesus is a Davidic Messiah, then Judas is an Absalomic betrayer."[3]

In Luke, the emphasis is on Judas' blood spilled on the ground. The money from Judas' betrayal of Jesus was used to purchase a plot of ground. Bejon thinks this might parallel the story of Ahab, king of Israel, who killed Naboth to acquire the latter's vineyard (1 Kgs 21). Because of his wickedness, Ahab is judged by God and dies a violent and bloody death. Bejon observes:

> The parallels between Judas's and Ahab's lives are important for a further reason. Insofar as Luke invites us to view Judas's death in light of Ahab's, he invites us to view Jesus' death in light of Naboth's, which is highly instructive. Like Naboth, Jesus is a faithful witness. He maintains his integrity in the face of a corrupt regime. He is the owner of a vineyard (Israel!). He is slandered by two false witnesses at a hurriedly convened religious event. And he's led outside a capital city by his accusers, where he's put to an ignominious death.[4]

We don't know for certain if Matthew and Luke had these parallels in mind, but the comparison is instructive nonetheless. Judas seems to embody some of the worst scumbags of the Old Testament. His betrayal stands in stark contrast to Jesus' faithfulness.

BETRAYAL THAT LEADS TO DEATH

Having followed Jesus during the years of his ministry, Judas got the opportunity to know the true Jesus—the sinless man, the glorious God, the authoritative teacher, the healer of both body and soul. Judas' guilt got the best of him. Upon seeing Jesus condemned, Judas seems to have grown a conscience. A momentous burden of guilt weighed him down, guilt that led him to take his own life. Matthew 27:3 tells us he "changed his mind." The Greek verb *metameletheis* used by Matthew carries connotations of repentance and regret. Herein lies the question: When Judas changed his mind, did he truly repent? It doesn't appear he did.

3. Bejon, "Judas's Demise."
4. Ibid.

Context is our clue to Judas' fate. Repentance denotes a change of direction. Repentance is what characterized the life of the tax collector Zacchaeus, who upon encountering Jesus, recognized his own need for salvation, publicly confessed his sin, and paid back everyone he had cheated (Luke 19:1–10). Repentance can be an emotionally difficult step to take. It can be embarrassing to acknowledge hidden sin. It can be life-altering to abandon lifestyle choices that have accompanied us for years or even decades. But true repentance is life-giving. To turn from death-inducing sin and to embrace the restoration and healing of new life, this is what lies at the heart of true repentance. I suspect a repentant Judas would have desperately returned to the Christ he betrayed, throwing himself at the feet of Jesus, pleading for mercy, and experiencing the joy of grace.

Judas wasn't repentant. He appears to exhibit only regret—in this case a kind of self-focused sorrow where we kick ourselves for messing up and wallow in self-pity. Unlike repentance that leads to life, unchecked regret leads to despair. Guilt and regret can drive a person mad with visions of their mistakes and no hope of reparation. One might imagine Shakespeare's Lady MacBeth walking the candle-lit halls of her castle by night, lamenting her implication in the regicide of King Duncan, rubbing the imaginary blood from her hands, and crying, "Out, damn spot, out I say!" One might imagine Judas doing likewise. His action doesn't bear the marks of a life restored, but the guilt of his own kind of regicide—the death of the King of kings.

LOYALTY THAT LEADS TO LIFE

Sometimes light appears brighter against a backdrop of darkness. The pain of treachery makes us appreciate faithfulness all the more. When we've experienced the bitterness of betrayal, the sweetness of absolute loyalty tastes a little better. Among other things, Judas' betrayal of Jesus serves to highlight the faithfulness of Jesus, even as he faced his darkest hour.

Even as the hour of his death approached, Jesus remained loyal to the Father's will, loyal to his mission, and loyal to his disciples. John 13:1–2 contrasts Judas' betrayal with Jesus' faithfulness when it says of Jesus: "Having loved his own who were in the world, he loved them to the end." In other words, he loved his disciples by laying down his life for them. He loved Thomas, who doubted him (John 20:24–9). He loved James and John, who quarreled over who would sit at his right and left hand (Mark 10:35–45).

He loved Matthew, the corrupt former IRS agent and sinner (Matt 9:9–13). He loved Peter, who said a lot of stupid things and acted like an ass on numerous occasions. The point is, Jesus loved this ragtag group of boneheads. He loved them in their ignorance. He loved them in their brokenness. He loved them when they quarreled or when they made outrageous requests.

The faithfulness of Jesus is captured in the parable of the lost sheep (Matt 18:10–4). He seeks and saves the lost . . . even if it means pursuing a solitary stray. He doesn't lose a single one entrusted to his eternal care (John 6:35–40). He pursues them. John 21 recounts how Jesus reinstated Peter after Peter's threefold public denial of his lord and savior. Notice the contrast between Peter and Judas. When Judas realized what he had done to Jesus, he fled from the Christ and hanged himself. He moved away from Jesus, alienating himself from life. In contrast, when Peter realized his denial, he ran, or literally swam, toward Jesus in repentance (John 21:7). In John 21, as the resurrected Jesus stands on the shore, Peter jumps from his boat like an excited child and swims to the shore in anticipation of seeing his friend. I suspect Peter wasn't certain if he would encounter rebuke, correction, gentleness, forgiveness, or something else. But he knew he needed Jesus. He flung himself into the path of redemption.

As Jesus received Peter and countered Peter's threefold denial with a threefold request for Peter's devotion, Jesus ends his reinstatement of Peter with the invitation, "Follow me" (John 21:19). Ironically, some of Jesus' final words to Peter mirror his initial words to Peter spoken years before, when Jesus first called him (Matt 4:19). His words convey the simple message: "I still want you with me."

> Follow me and I will make you a fisher of men. Follow me and I will make you a feeder of my sheep. Follow me, for I will never leave you nor forsake you. I will never betray my friends.

STUDY QUESTIONS

1. Think of a time you changed your mind about something important.

2. Read Matthew 27:3–10 and Acts 1:15–19. Who is Judas? What role did he play in the death of Jesus?

3. We read that Judas changed his mind and returned the blood money. Is there a difference between regret/remorse and repentance? Explain. (In other words, what characterizes repentance? Hope, desire for fellowship with God, etc.) Do you think Judas truly repented? Explain.

4. What apparent contradictions do you see between the two accounts? Is it possible to reconcile these differences?

5. People sometimes take their own lives for various reasons. Do you think suicide is an automatic ticket to eternal judgment? How might God's grace still abound in these difficult cases?

6. Read Matthew 26:20–25. If God knew Judas would betray the Messiah, and had prepared this event in advance, did Judas have a choice in the matter? How does God's sovereignty generally coincide with human choices and responsibilities?

7. Is there anything redeemable or positive that could possibly come from this account? How is God glorified through this events of Jesus' betrayal?

14

Death by Preaching — Acts 20

On the first day of the week, when we were gathered together to break bread, Paul talked with them, intending to depart on the next day, and he prolonged his speech until midnight. There were many lamps in the upper room where we were gathered. And a young man named Eutychus, sitting at the window, sank into a deep sleep as Paul talked still longer. And being overcome by sleep, he fell down from the third story and was taken up dead. But Paul went down and bent over him, and taking him in his arms, said, "Do not be alarmed, for his life is in him." And when Paul had gone up and had broken bread and eaten, he conversed with them a long while, until daybreak, and so departed. And they took the youth away alive, and were not a little comforted.

—Acts 20:6–12

TRADITIONAL WOODEN CHURCH PEWS are difficult to sit in, let alone sleep in. They're functional, utilitarian pieces of furniture. One might wonder if their uncomfortable design was intentional. If you're not comfortable, you'll be unable to sleep, and if you're unable to sleep, you'll be more likely to hear the message, which increases the likelihood you'll receive the message. We could reason that uncomfortable wooden pews are an odd means of grace—a divinely appointed instrument of pain that spiritually fortifies the recipient. In essence, hard wooden pews are good for your soul.

The wooden pew is but one of many creative mechanisms employed by imaginative pastors, reverends, vicars, and priests to keep their parishioners awake. In addition, pulpit pounding has been effectively employed by many impassioned preachers to startle dozing congregants. Furthermore, the promise of a sip of communion wine for those who endure the sermon might just keep others from nodding off. Liturgical churches use frequent standing and sitting to effectively prevent dozing and promote heart-healthy calisthenics. Loud worship music, audio-visual displays, coffee, and awkward meet-and-greet times also play their part in contributing to attentive listeners.

I've had the pleasure of preaching quite a few sermons over the years. No matter the size of the church, I usually catch someone sleeping through my stirring and compelling messages. I guess I'm in good company. The apostle Paul put people to sleep as well. His preaching even killed someone once. That's actually pretty cool. Some kid was so bored to death by Paul's incessant bloviating that he went into a narcoleptic fit of sleep-shock and dove headlong out a window just to escape the bore-fest.

While playing the word game of *Balderdash* with my family recently, I came across the word *scaldabanco*, which apparently refers to a stirring, engaging, and fiery preacher. Paul was not a scaldabanco. Paul was a scholar and lecturer. I don't think preaching was his strength. He even says of himself: "Even if I am unskilled in speaking, I am not so in knowledge" (2 Cor 11:6). He knew his limits and trusted God to be his strength in weakness.

These days, preachers find it difficult to compete with all the incredible entertainment options we have available to us. People are easily bored. Good preachers become mediocre preachers compared to the impressive specimens found on the internet. I don't envy preachers who compete every Sunday with better rehearsed, more winsome, more attractive, better dressed, better coiffed, better paid rock star preachers. Well-meaning churchgoers love to counsel the ordinary, dull, and common preachers on how to make the message more compelling. In spite of the hours of study, prayer, and reflection that go into a pastor's sermon preparation, others with little background and little tact will happily provide unsolicited theological and pastoral "advice." I'm sure many seasoned pastors have learned the art of smiling and politely thanking these dear, well-intentioned "experts," for their profound insights.

So, what's the point of the story of poor Eutychus falling asleep in church? I suppose we could say the moral of the story might be: Don't play near open windows (see the story of Jezebel in 2 Kgs 9). Or, we could speculate that the moral is: Don't fall asleep in church. We might even add: Avoid boring, longwinded preachers who like to hear themselves talk. But I suspect there might be a more important message hidden in Acts 20: The preaching of God's word is a matter of life and death.

THE POWER OF THE WORD

Eutychus was a typical teenager who liked video games, pizza, and rolling his eyes at his parents. He had too much homework and not enough sleep. So, when his parents dragged him to a meet-and-greet with the Amazing Dr. Paul the apostle, he figured he would be in for a long night. Luckily, he had his smartphone to keep him entertained while he sprawled languidly in the window alcove. Unluckily, his phone ran out of battery about two hours into Paul's academic discourse on the varying interpretations of the trinitarian controversy over eternal functional subordination. "This sucks," thought Eutychus as he looked around the room for a wall outlet where he could charge his phone. There was none to be found. After an eternity elapsed, he finally resigned himself to accept his current situation. Eutychus did his best to listen. Surprisingly, he even learned some interesting stuff. This whole Jesus movement was actually pretty cool. But all things considered, you have to grant that none of us would be doing well after five or six hours of lecturing, even if the lectures are brought to you courtesy of the Amazing Dr. Paul.

The weary youth began to nod off. Soon, he was sound asleep. Next thing he knew he was dreaming that he was riding a unicorn across a rainbow. Then the rainbow disappeared, and he found himself sitting in a pub in Wales playing cards with a one-eyed sea captain named Harold. As he dreamed on, he was suddenly being chased through the woods by a pack of ravenous wolves. Turning to look back at his pursuers, his foot slipped, and he began the plummet from an insanely high cliff. Turns out, that part wasn't a dream. He never woke up. His mangled body lay in a heap on the cobblestones below.

Meanwhile, Paul, annoyed by the interruption, stopped his lecture so everyone could take a bathroom break and get a cup of coffee. The line for the bathroom was too long, so while he waited, Paul went down to the street to revive the dead adolescent. The apostle casually stuffed Eutychus's brain back into his head, raised him from the dead, gave him a Red Bull energy drink so it wouldn't happen again, and told everyone to get back up to the apartment so he could finish part thirty-seven of his stirring message on penal substitutionary atonement in pre-Levitical Abrahamic covenantal theology.

The irony of the whole situation is that *Eutychus* means "fortunate," or "of good fortune." I guess when all was said and done, he was truly fortunate to be restored to life. The miracle is a critical piece of the story. But there's more. Even more exciting than the raising of Eutychus is the beautiful fellowship that took place in this home. All joking aside, Paul's "speech" was life-giving. These new Christians needed to be fed the nourishing word of God. They longed for instruction, communion, fellowship, and the comfort of the Lord.

We read that Paul's *logos*, or speech, extended on and on. And this logos (word) was undoubtedly about *the* Logos (Jesus Christ). In fact, in John's gospel account, the logos refers to Jesus himself. Jesus, the Word made flesh, is God's ultimate and final revelation. It's no coincidence that Jesus is referred to as the Word. The idea of language, speech, words, and propositional truth is critical to the Christian religion. The content of the message matters. The substance of the message matters. The truth of the message matters. The person to whom the message points matters.

ALSO, THE POWER OF THE WORD

Preaching is about life and death. It's more important today than ever. It will continue to be more important than ever. Throw out whatever else you want from church, but don't take the critical and essential proclamation of the gospel. The most famous of all preachers, Charles Spurgeon, once said, "Let the sun stop shining, and we will preach in darkness. Let the waves stop their ebb and flow, and still our voice shall preach the gospel." I'll add this: Let the world complain and deride the preaching of the word as a useless, time-wasting activity, and still we must preach all the more fervently. The word of God must be preached. Paul's charge to his young protégé, Timothy, is worth quoting at length:

> Preach the word; be ready in season and out of season; reprove, rebuke, and exhort, with complete patience and teaching. For the time is coming when people will not endure sound teaching, but

having itching ears they will accumulate for themselves teachers to suit their own passions, and will turn away from listening to the truth and wander off into myths. As for you, always be sober-minded, endure suffering, do the work of an evangelist, fulfill your ministry (2 Tim 4:2–5).

Christian preachers preach to glorify God in proclaiming the truth. Preaching affords the church the opportunity to verbally acknowledge the wonders and majesty of God. To preach is to proclaim that there is truth worth hearing—life-giving, soul-awakening, joy-inducing truth. The truth-giver, God, is glorified when we speak the truth in love and proclaim the truth of the gospel that Jesus Christ gave his life on behalf of a fallen human race, that by faith the fallen would be raised up to life.

Preaching is the ordinary means by which Christians announce the gospel of salvation to the lost. God ordained that the proclamation of the word would lead to repentance. In Acts 2, the apostle Peter stood up in the power of the Holy Spirit and gave a compelling sermon, walking step by step through Scripture, and proving that Jesus is the Christ. The people's response to the preaching of the word was to collectively cry out: "What shall we do?" (Acts 2:37). Peter's response: "Repent!" Believe the gospel and be baptized in the name of the Father, Son, and Holy Spirit. After all, how will they believe unless the gospel is preached (Rom 10:14)?

We preach to remember who God is and what God requires of us. Christians need the gospel every day. We can't live without it. It's life! It's breath! It's that which compels us to walk in obedience to the Lord. We need to be reminded each and every day to submit ourselves to God, lest we succumb to the world, the flesh, and the devil (Eph 2:1–3). My unsolicited advice to the church would be this: preach the person and work of Christ to one another one more time. Then, after you've preached it, preach it again. Bathe in it. Saturate yourself in it. Listen to it on repeat. Get to know your God. It will only help you love him more. Get to know your Lord. It will only help you serve him better.

Christians must preach and hear preaching so they can grow in faith and knowledge of God. We preach and are preached to in pursuit of relationship with God. Preaching is not about gaining insight into some abstract and esoteric knowledge of the cosmos. Preaching is about a person—the God of the universe, the creator and savior of the world, the judge and redeemer. The central purpose of preaching is that we would be led to know God and align our hearts to him. Tim Keller aptly noted: "A good sermon is not like a club that beats upon the will but like a sword that cuts to the heart."[1] The preaching of the word of God gets our heart beating in tune to him.

John Calvin is said to have practically died preaching. Toward the end of his life, when he was too weak to walk to the church to proclaim the wonders of God, he was carried in his chair. He didn't want God to return and find him idly wasting away in bed. On his deathbed, his friends pleaded with him to cease his labors. He replied: "What! Would you have the Lord find me idle when he comes?"[2] He would die preaching. I like that. Maybe Eutychus didn't have it so bad after all. If we're going to die, let it be while preaching or being preached to. Let's encourage each other one more time with the story of Jesus Christ.

STUDY QUESTIONS

1. What technique do you find most effective when you really need to stay awake?

2. Read Acts 20:6–12. Who are all the characters in the story? Where are they? What are they doing?

3. Why do you suppose Paul kept talking so late into the night? Imagine the content of his speech. What was so important that he kept talking?

4. What became of Eutychus during the course of Paul's speech? Does the death of Eutychus seem to disrupt Paul's sermon? Does this tell us anything about the importance of the preaching of the word and the power of the word?

1. Keller, *Preaching*, 21.
2. Beza, *Life of John Calvin*, 84.

5. In the story, Paul's longwinded "words," coupled with Eutychus's fatigue brought death. Yet, everyone left encouraged or "comforted." Where do we see irony in this story?

6. Read 1 Peter 1:22–25. How is the word of God alive? How is it alive in you today?

7. Think about the power of words in your own life. When have the words of others brought comfort and growth? When have the words of others torn you down and hurt you?

8. Is there an area in your life now, where words of truth and love need to be spoken by you or to you?

9. Do we take the preaching of the word seriously enough in the church today? Explain. In what areas of your life do you need to wake up and hear what God is saying to you?

10. How can we be more effective in the preaching of the word and the reception of the message?

15

Severed Head — Mark 6

King Herod heard of it, for Jesus' name had become known. Some said, "John the Baptist has been raised from the dead. That is why these miraculous powers are at work in him." But others said, "He is Elijah." And others said, "He is a prophet, like one of the prophets of old." But when Herod heard of it, he said, "John, whom I beheaded, has been raised." For it was Herod who had sent and seized John and bound him in prison for the sake of Herodias, his brother Philip's wife, because he had married her. For John had been saying to Herod, "It is not lawful for you to have your brother's wife." And Herodias had a grudge against him and wanted to put him to death. But she could not, for Herod feared John, knowing that he was a righteous and holy man, and he kept him safe. When he heard him, he was greatly perplexed, and yet he heard him gladly.

But an opportunity came when Herod on his birthday gave a banquet for his nobles and military commanders and the leading men of Galilee. For when Herodias's daughter came in and danced, she pleased Herod and his guests. And the king said to the girl, "Ask me for whatever you wish, and I will give it to you." And he vowed to her, "Whatever you ask me, I will give you, up to half of my kingdom." And she went out and said to her mother, "For what should I ask?" And she said, "The head of John the Baptist." And she came in immediately with haste to the king and asked, saying, "I want you to give me at once the head of John the Baptist on a platter." And the king was exceedingly sorry, but because of his oaths and his guests he did not want to break his word to her. And immediately the king sent an executioner with orders to bring John's head. He went and beheaded him in the prison and brought his head on a platter and gave it to the girl, and the girl gave it to her mother. When his disciples heard of it, they came and took his body and laid it in a tomb.

—Mark 6:14–29

THE TITLE OF THIS chapter sounds like the name of a Swedish death metal band, whose music video for their latest EP, *Unholy Pestilential Abscess of Fiendish Grave Desecration*, has garnered a mixed response from fans on YouTube. If a band called *Severed Head* doesn't already exist, I would strongly urge someone to start one immediately. It's too good a name to pass up . . . and it's biblical.

John the Baptist lost his head for speaking the truth—not just *his* truth, but *the* truth. Clearly truth was no less controversial in John's day than it is today. But truth matters and we must stand firm in it even if that means losing our reputation, our standing in society, or our head.

Historically, beheadings have been a standard form of execution. Severed heads tend to show up more frequently during times of war. Mounting the heads of your slain enemies on a pole is a great way to tell everyone you mean business. Drug cartels use this method to strike fear into the hearts of contenders and defectors. The French had a period in their history where they really got into the whole decapitation thing. Anyone who gave off the slightest hint of aristocratic attachment was promptly guillotined. In fact, guillotines were used for executions in France until 1977. Other cultures prefer to hack heads off with machetes or other fearsome weapons. We've all heard stories of decapitations at the hands of Islamic extremists. In the first couple of decades post 9/11, such executions were commonplace. Even back in the good old days, invaders would catapult severed heads over Medieval walled cities during assaults on enemy fortified positions. At least, I saw something like that in a movie once. It must be true. Before we figured out democracy, it used to be that instead of voting a person out of office, we would just decapitate them and replace them with someone else. King Charles I of England might know something about that . . . so would Louis XVI. Those were simpler times.

People who wanted to keep their heads stayed out of politics. Saying the wrong thing to the wrong person could get you in trouble. Speaking the truth to the wrong person could get you dead. This is especially true of biblical prophets who just can't keep their mouths shut. Prophets like to show up uninvited and point out the sins of kings and nations. This is the mistake John the Baptist made. He called out Herod's sin and was thrown in prison for his lack of diplomacy. Later, Herod's wife got her meat hooks on him and took his head.

John the Baptist was an interesting character. Now, you're probably wondering why he was called "John the Baptist." Why not John the Presbyterian, or John the Episcopalian? Why not John the Unitarian Universalist? Well, John was a *baptizer* who used to rove the desert region near the Jordan River calling the people to repentance. The apostle Matthew describes him as being clothed in camel hair (Matt 3:4). I imagine him in a camel skin onesie, with the camel head as a hood and a cute camel tail hanging out the back. It was an elaborate, if not adorable, Halloween costume. Besides baptizing people in the Jordan river, John survived in the desert on a diet of calorie-dense honey and protein-rich locusts. Fried, roasted, sauteed, or baked, it didn't matter. John knew how to enjoy a good wild locust.

It's reasonable to classify John as the last of the Old Testament prophets. He came as "the voice of one crying in the wilderness: 'Prepare the way of the Lord; make his paths straight'" (Matt 3:3; Isa 40:3). He called the people to repentance as he announced the coming of the savior of the people of Israel. He also told Herod Antipas (not to be confused with Herod the Great, Herod Agrippa I or Herod Agrippa II) to stop being an immoral scoundrel for running off with Herodias, his sister-in-law, who was also his niece. Yes, it's weird. John the "Baptist" and "Investigative Journalist" was not discreet in publicly calling out Herod's sin and writing editorials about corrupt politicians, which angered Herodias. She didn't like to see her face on the front page of the local tabloids.

John ended up in the clink where he awaited his fate. He kept busy trading cigarettes, played cards, and starting a gang. Prison, however, did not stop him from preaching and prophesying, to the chagrin of his cell mates. He just kept telling Herod he was an idiot and a miserable wretched sinner. Herod didn't seem to mind the criticism. Mark's account of the story tells us that Herod was "perplexed" but heard John's preaching "gladly" (Mark 6:20). All the while, Herodias was looking for a reason to have John executed. She got her chance at Herod's birthday celebration.

THE DANGERS OF SPEAKING THE TRUTH

We don't know exact details, but I'll risk a little speculation of how things played out in Mark 6. For Herod's birthday, his wife organized an extravagant soirée. The catering service was top notch—French fusion with a touch of California chic. Cases of Cristal were unloaded into the bar where they were put on ice. A local DJ, Professor Doctor Jedidiah Funk-Surgeon, General Practitioner of Downbeat, ensured the guests would linger well into the night. It was a beautiful evening. Stars filled the night sky. The lighting and décor were perfect. There were plenty of celebrities and attractive socialites milling about. It was a typical rich-guy party. As the evening progressed and the wine flowed, drunken guests danced, laughed, and behaved lasciviously. Herod was loving every minute of it.

As the haunting sounds of lyre and flute resonated through the palace, the evening's special entertainment began. Royal dancers in varying states of undress moved seductively among the guests. But who was that mysterious young woman who emerged from the corner of the room and joined in the dance? Beneath the dusky lights she conveyed her lithe body effortlessly. Lustful eyes followed her movements. Lush of hip and heavy of breast, she was a true beauty. She moved her lissome body invitingly into Herod's view. Her Versace halter evening gown left little to the imagination as she danced bewitchingly, fully intent on widening eyes and inciting dreams.

Korasion is the Greek word for girl used in Mark 6. It can refer to a maiden or unmarried girl. Like its English equivalent, *korasion* can refer to a child and young adult. However, if we consider Herod's character, the kinds of dinner guests present, and the fact that Herodias seems to have sent the girl with the intention to please the guests and garner Herod's favor, the context suggests the dance was probably intended to be sexual in nature.[1] This was not a cute six-year-old who came in to perform the *Dance of the Sugarplum Fairy*. This was more akin to some wild pole dancing action.

Herod couldn't restrain himself. When finally their eyes met, he motioned her over to join him on his lavish couch, shooing his consorts away. With his arm around the girl's shoulder, the dirty old man whispered in her ear. She flirted back. He repeated his drunken advances. Enamored with the girl, Herod offered her opulent gifts. "Anything your heart desires, even up to half my kingdom."

---

1. Commentating on Mark 6:21–3, Walter Wessel, suggests "the danse was probably a lewd one." Wessel, *Mark*, 670.

Once spoken, his words could not be repealed. No doubt Herod secretly hoped his promise would go unfulfilled. But things had been set in motion that couldn't be undone. There are three reasons Herod got here: 1) The girl was extremely attractive, 2) Herod was extremely drunk, or 3) the girl was extremely attractive *and* Herod was extremely drunk. Let's assume the third the most likely of the three. Let's also pause to acknowledge the weirdness of the situation. Remember that Herod had unlawfully taken his brother Philip's wife in marriage. If the girl was Herod's brother's former wife's daughter, this would have made her his niece. The whole affair hints at scandal and perversion.

What could a girl who has everything possibly want? A pony? A pretty gold necklace? A trip to Disney World? She consulted her mother. Herodias thought for a moment. Then it came to her. A devious smile broke her pensive glare. "Ask for the head of John the Baptist." Herod immediately regretted his generous offer, as made clear by the narrative of Mark 6. Nonetheless, his honor required him to *execute* his promise. John was brought out posthaste and beheaded. The lurid trophy was put on a platter and presented to the girl like the main dish of a multicourse dinner. "Voila madame, le plat principal!"

There's at least one moral of this story: Don't make promises you're not prepared to keep; don't get mixed up with bad company; don't attend wild parties; don't hang out with prophets. But the main point might be more subtle: There are sometimes consequences to speaking the truth. John was executed for saying the *right* thing to the *wrong* person. Mark 6 never tells exactly what John said or the tone in which it was said. Truth can be communicated harshly or winsomely, with good motives or bad. It can be handed down as an angry rebuke, or as a kind and gentle plea to step back into the light. No doubt, John, a prophet of God, spoke with conviction and authority. He spoke the truth to those who desperately needed it.

TRUTH IN CONTEMPORARY CULTURE

Truth has fallen out of fashion in our broader culture. Truth has also fallen out of fashion in the church. Contemporary church culture seems increasingly enamored with doubt, deconstruction, skepticism, and half-truth. Progressive Christianity is all the rage. By *progressive*, I'm not just referring to people who appreciate the nuance and complexities involved in careful biblical reflection and who are willing to enter into serious dialogue with others. Instead, this movement of thought is characterized by suspicion of perceived antiquated notions of biblical authority, distrust of traditional views of sexuality and gender, and skepticism regarding objective mind-independent truth that corresponds to reality. Progressive Christianity is suspicious of the doctrine of hell, and accepts universalist notions of salvation. The exclusive claims of Jesus are seen as narrow-minded.

Those with progressive sympathies will often reject the progressive label as a meaningless or unhelpful term. They will likely call for more nuance, more open-mindedness, and less doctrine. Their views spring from legitimate felt concerns, questions, and observations about Christianity that bring them discomfort and that have alienated them from the more conservative branches of Evangelical Christianity. I worry, however, that those with progressive leanings have succumbed to a false gospel, replete with a deficient view of the truth of the death and resurrection of Jesus and the need to hold fast to this reality.

I worry that those who lean into progressive views have unduly let truth fall to the wayside. Aligning themselves with religious skeptics, they miss the sweetness of the gospel and its transformative effect. They have more in common with the world than with the church. Oddly and sadly, those with progressive leanings often treat truth like some nefarious force on the polar opposite of love. It's as if truth and love are in conflict—bad on one side, good on the other; cerebral nonsense on one side, heart on the other. But the Bible teaches that love speaks the language of truth by rejoicing in the truth (1 Cor 13:6). Likewise, when truth speaks, it must be motivated by love for the purpose of building up God's people (Eph 4:15). Truth and love exist in an intimate bond. Christians are called to be truth-speakers. They are also called to be truth-hearers.

The members of Herod's household responded to truth in varying, but insufficient, ways. Herod was ambivalent to the truth. He listened to John and walked away unchanged. In a way, Herod is the guy who shows up to church to happily sing worship songs and take copious sermon notes, but who can't get the truth from his head to his heart. Herod is like the seed sown along the path in Jesus' parable of the sower (Mark 4). Some seed was scattered on the path where the birds swept down and snatched it away. Herod lacked a receptacle to catch and retain the truth. Because his heart is not prepared to cultivate the word, and because his mind is not equipped to curate knowledge of God, he heard the truth and walked away unchanged.

Herod's wife . . . niece . . . sister-in-law, or whatever she was, was hostile to the truth. Where Herod couldn't receive the truth, Herodias hated the truth. She was hell-bent on silencing the truth. She was like a first-century version of the cancel culture that plagues the West in these early decades of the twenty-first century. To cancel someone is to crush them—to remove them from public discourse—to silence them, to ruin them, and to blot out their words and their ability to speak those words. Rather than responding to disagreements through rational discourse and respectful correction, cancelation seeks to silence people and eliminate their participation in society. Often, cancelation is inflicted for minor offenses. Herodias canceled John definitively and brutally.

Finally, Herod's other niece—his stepdaughter, the girl—played the role of a willing pawn in the whole vile affair. Lacking a solid moral foundation, she simply let herself be swayed by others and blown by the winds, waves, and whims of the wicked. She was led by lies. When we're not listening to the right voices, we can easily be swayed by the wrong ones.

In this battle for the truth, two kingdoms are in conflict. The kingdom of Herod, planted in the soil of vanity and excess, produced a rotten crop that detracted from the life-giving truth that leads to human flourishing. It was an earthly kingdom, marked by political maneuvering, power struggles, and strife. The kingdom of God was different (John 18:36). This kingdom, announced by John and inaugurated by Jesus, did not give heed to the empty promises of power. Its struggle was not against flesh and blood (Eph. 6:12). God's kingdom is not about controlling a scrap of real estate. It's about the redemptive rule of Christ. King Jesus opens the eyes of the blind, giving light and color where there was none before (John 9:1–7). He sees the unseen and touches the unclean (Mark 1:40–42). He stares down death and defies its cold lifeless grasp as he calls the dead out of their tombs (John 11). King Jesus atones for sin in a decisive victory over sin, the devil, and the grave. He sets the world on a path toward healing. He teaches us truth that sets us free (John 8:31–32).

When God's prophets and apostles speak truth, it is out of love for God and with love for God's people. Often this truth is hard to swallow. In the introduction to his book *Truth Decay*, Douglas Groothuis says this of truth:

> Truth is a daunting, difficult thing; it is also the greatest thing in the world. Yet we are chronically ambivalent toward it. We seek it . . . and we fear it. Our better side wants to pursue truth wherever

it leads; our darker side balks when the truth begins to lead us anywhere we do not want to go. Let the truth be damned if the truth would damn us![2]

Groothuis has identified a fundamental human discomfort with truth. Truth is like a spotlight that exposes us as criminals with flawed views and deficient understanding. But fortunately, truth is also a searchlight fixed on us when we are lost in a dark wilderness. It's our salvation. Whether we like the truth or not is irrelevant. Truth enjoys an intimate relationship with reality.

The truth-reality relationship is sometimes called the correspondence theory of truth, or the classical theory of truth. Philosophers, William Lane Craig and J.P. Moreland, offer that the correspondence theory of truth "is a matter a proposition (belief, thought, statement, representation) corresponding to reality."[3] Alisa Childers adds this concerning truth:

> Some think it's just a subjective opinion or preference, much like your favorite sport, movie, or candy bar. But the definition of truth is actually quite simple: Truth is a thought, statement, or opinion that lines up with reality.[4]

People of God should be people of truth—seeking truth, knowing truth, and living out truth. God's people should be committed to joining truth to love as we orient our goals toward gospel proclamation and gospel transformation. Truth can be spoken loudly, gently, winsomely, or passionately and still be spoken lovingly.

Truth-tellers are people who care about reality and want others to care as well. And the most important reality we could ever care about is our relationship to God. Relating to God correctly means being truthful about our faults and truthful about our need for a savior. As a truth-teller, not only did John the Baptist call out Herod's sin, he announced a solution to sin—Jesus Christ, the way, the truth, and the life (John 14:6). Winsome truth-tellers and humble truth-seekers are needed in this world.

2. Groothuis, *Truth Decay*, 9.
3. Craig and Moreland, *Philosophical Foundations*, 130.
4. Childers, *Live Your Truth and Other Lies*, 25.

STUDY QUESTIONS

1. Think of a time when telling the truth got you into trouble.

2. Read Mark 6:14–29 (and Matt 3:1–6). Who was John the Baptist? What was his unique calling from God? Why did Herod have him arrested?

3. What was Herod's overall reaction to John and his teaching? What do you think caused Herod to fear John? What brought about the death of John?

4. John wasn't afraid to call out the sin of the leaders around him. Are we afraid to call out lies and sin among our own leaders in the church and society? Is there a right way to speak truth? What are the risks of truth-speaking today?

5. What are the biggest lies and sins in our contemporary society that seem to be off limits to truth-speakers?

6. Has anyone ever "called you out"? Did it make you angry, or did you end up respecting that person more? Explain.

7. Herod seems to have made a hasty and foolish promise. Have you ever done the same?

8. Read John 8:31–2. What does the truth of who Jesus is change in us?

16

Cruel Stonework — Acts 6 and 7

And Stephen, full of grace and power, was doing great wonders and signs among the people. Then some of those who belonged to the synagogue of the Freedmen (as it was called), and of the Cyrenians, and of the Alexandrians, and of those from Cilicia and Asia, rose up and disputed with Stephen. But they could not withstand the wisdom and the Spirit with which he was speaking. Then they secretly instigated men who said, "We have heard him speak blasphemous words against Moses and God." And they stirred up the people and the elders and the scribes, and they came upon him and seized him and brought him before the council, and they set up false witnesses who said, "This man never ceases to speak words against this holy place and the law, for we have heard him say that this Jesus of Nazareth will destroy this place and will change the customs that Moses delivered to us." And gazing at him, all who sat in the council saw that his face was like the face of an angel.

—Acts 6:8–15

Now when they heard these things they were enraged, and they ground their teeth at him. But he, full of the Holy Spirit, gazed into heaven and saw the glory of God, and Jesus standing at the right hand of God. And he said, "Behold, I see the heavens opened, and the Son of Man standing at the right hand of God." But they cried out with a loud voice and stopped their ears and rushed together at

him. Then they cast him out of the city and stoned him. And the witnesses laid
down their garments at the feet of a young man named Saul. And as they were
stoning Stephen, he called out, "Lord Jesus, receive my spirit." And falling to his
knees he cried out with a loud voice, "Lord, do not hold this sin against them."
And when he had said this, he fell asleep.

—ACTS 7:54–60

WHEN YOU'RE IN A debate and you're unable to offer a well-thought-out
or coherent rational argument for your viewpoint, here are several time-
tested and proven methods to ensure you come out on top.

First, insult your opponent rather than addressing their arguments
in an honest and forthright manner. This will draw attention away from
your inability to respond cogently to their views. Find something about the
person's appearance, mannerisms, and speech that you can publicly dispar-
age. Once you've identified these weaknesses, utilize a barrage of insults,
while sneering, laughing, shaking your head in disbelief at their stupidity.
Try also punctuating your insults with low-decibel mutterings under your
breath.

Second, yell and talk over your opponent. The distraction will prevent
them from being able to focus and defend their views. This method will
also demonstrate your superior social prowess and mastery of the art of
rhetoric and communication. Noise always triumphs over reason.

Third, claim that your opponent's views are threatening to your mental
health. Their worldview and opinions have induced psychological trauma
and caused irreversible damage to your emotional state. Cry, convulse, and
roll on the floor in a fit of outrage. Demand a safe space where you can
grieve in a protected environment. Lock yourself in a sheltered area where
all the big bad mean true rational ideas can't get you. Get angry. Get emotional. Don't underestimate the effectiveness of the tried and true temper
tantrum—the conniption fit.

Once you've exhausted these options, a final, drastic approach should
be considered. In cases where insults and general obnoxiousness fail to produce the desired results, try taking physical action against your opponent
by beating them, stabbing them, or if possible, shooting them. This is a
surefire way to maintain the upper hand in an argument. In the name of all

that is good and civil and appropriate, kill the bastards who disagree with you.

Many people have used the above methods effectively throughout history. Just look at modern day university campuses, where the slightest divergence from the outrageous extreme secular status quo will get you publicly destroyed. Just look at poor Stephen in Acts 7. Stephen got on the wrong side of a bunch of nut jobs when he claimed that Jesus was the savior of the world, and that people should repent and put their faith in God. Some people didn't want to hear it, so they entered into a debate with Stephen. The problem with this approach was that Stephen was smarter than them. So, they tried to accuse him of being a jerk. The problem with that approach was that Stephen was nicer than them. Then they tried being godlier and more righteous than Stephen. Once again this didn't work. Stephen was filled with the Holy Spirit. What were these guys supposed to do? Finally, they decided to just kill him and have the whole thing over with.

It worked! They dragged him out of the city and threw a bunch of heavy rocks on him until he died of blunt force trauma. Now that's how you win a debate!

The story of Stephen's martyrdom shows how ideological bias deafens our ability to hear any possible corrective. Stephen's death also reminds us of the offensiveness of the gospel. The message of the gospel offends our pride. It offends our self-sufficiency. It offends our inclination to be our own god. That's the problem with Christianity. You see, most other religions allow you to be your own god by taking your salvation into your own hands and working your way to heaven by praying, meditating, observing laws, and performing various works of righteousness. If you want to be saved, save yourself. Christianity, on the contrary, teaches the opposite: If you want to be saved, let Jesus save you.

THE FOOLISHNESS OF THE WISDOM OF THE WORLD

Appointed by the apostles to care for the daily needs of the early Christian community, Stephen was known as a *deacon*, or servant, of the church. He was also a fiery preacher who was filled with the Holy Spirit and who could perform cool signs and wonders, like healing the sick and casting devils out of people Van Helsing-style.

Because of Stephen's teaching about the lordship of Jesus, and because God was behind everything Stephen was able to do, people got jealous. It's kind of like when you think you're good at basketball, but then someone else shows up, and they're a lot better at basketball. They're not mean about it. They don't rub it in your face. They might even give you some pointers. But they're still annoying. If you think you're the best, nothing they do, or don't do, matters. You hate them on sight and sound. You want to be them, and you want them to fail at the same time. That's kind of how jealousy works.

Now, I don't know how tactful Stephen was in his teaching. I can't say I disagree with anything he said. After all, his speech was inspired by the Holy Spirit. His intent was to call his peers to repent of their sin and believe in Jesus as Israel's promised messiah. On the other hand, it probably didn't help his cause when he accused the Jewish authorities (Sanhedrin) of being "stiff-necked," hard-hearted, God-resisting murderers (Acts 7:51–3). This isn't generally how we win friends and influence people, especially in the context of a court of law.

Stephen told the religious and civil authorities of the day that they were ignorant of God. They wouldn't recognize God if he jumped out and kicked them in the face. They wouldn't recognize him if he showed up, took on human flesh and nature, performed a bunch of miracles, physically rose from the dead, then ascended into heaven in front of a whole bunch of witnesses. Stephen's sermon was an epic, face-melting speech. But the Sanhedrin was more interested in what they said about God, than what God said about himself. These jerks wouldn't listen to God's prophets. They wouldn't listen to the Son of God, their own Messiah. So, it's understandable they weren't going to listen to a mere deacon of the church who apparently had a cute angel face, or something to that affect, according to Acts 6:15.

Conventional human wisdom ended up prevailing—wisdom that said: "This guy opposes our authority, our status, our tradition, and our cool fancy robes. He doesn't know the secret password to our club (which was "New England clam chowder," in case you were wondering). He doesn't even know our secret handshake. Let's get him!" So, they covered their ears, and yelled, "lalala . . . blah, blah, blah . . . I'm not listening . . . lalala." Then they rushed toward Stephen like that army of grubby looking Scots in *Braveheart*. They dragged him outside Jerusalem and pummeled him with stones until he died.

As one would guess, stoning involved throwing rocks at the offender until the person was declared dead. In the Jewish Mishnah, which recounts the oral traditions of the Jewish people, an offender could be thrown down from a height of several body-lengths onto a bed of presumably jagged stones below (m. Kaetub. 4). If that didn't kill the offender, more stones were cast down on them until the job was done. The witnesses to the crime were often the first to throw stones at the accused (Deut 17:6–7). In the case of Stephen, *false* witnesses got this privilege.

Commentators note that at the moment of Stephen's martyrdom, Jesus is *standing* at the right hand of the Father (Acts 7:55). This is the only time in Scripture we're told Jesus was standing rather than sitting at the side of the Father. The ultimate judge and defense attorney, Jesus himself, was standing in defense of the accused.[1] And even if the wisdom of the world stood in accusation of Stephen, the wisdom of the ultimate judge stood to acquit and restore.

THE WISDOM OF THE FOOLISHNESS OF THE CROSS

Human wisdom fools us into thinking that without God's help we can know God and understand the mind of God, the plan of God, and the gospel of God. For the Sanhedrin human wisdom locked them into a particular way of doing things. They couldn't see that God was at work. Human wisdom leaves us unbalanced and blind to the extraordinary truths we might be missing. Human wisdom fools us into thinking our own experiences and insights serve us better than time-tested truth. It forces us into a very small box of our own making. It forces God into an even smaller box. Human wisdom writes a lopsided story of who God is and leaves us with a distorted gospel that stops short of God and his glory.

Conventional human wisdom trickles into biblical theology and subtly transforms the word of God into the word of man. Often human wisdom sounds good. Often it contains some half-truths and hints of biblical wisdom. Human wisdom says things like this:

- If you say the "sinner's prayer," you'll be magically saved and never have to worry about your spiritual life again.
- The gospel isn't about what you believe, it's about a relationship.
- Don't get too hung up on reading the Bible; that just makes Scripture into an idol.

1. See Sproul, *Acts*, 106–7.

- The problem with the Pharisees is that they were all knowledge and no heart.

- I don't need the church to have a relationship with God.

- Doctrine divides; convictions only tear the church apart.

- All sin is the same in the eyes of God.

- The God of the New Testament is so much more loving than the God of the Old Testament.

- You should never judge others or point out their sin.

- Live your truth.

- Whatever you feel is reality

With the most charitable reading I can muster, I'm willing to grant that these statements simply need some clarity, context, and correction. At worst, these vapid aphorisms are outrageous and destructive. They become a gospel according to Satan.[2] These remarks show up frequently in churches around the world.[3] They're often spoken in ignorance. They're rarely corrected for fear that the corrector might sound rude and holier than thou. One of the few heresies left in the contemporary church is the scandalous and blasphemous assertion that there even *is* such thing as heresy.

Honestly, today, sound biblical teaching might get you stoned . . . figuratively. To call out today's New Evangelical Christian Sanhedrin (as we'll call them) is to risk the accusation of being unloving and divisive. So what? Was Stephen a vitriolic maniac hellbent on tearing down God's people? No! He was filled with the Spirit and the word. Truth is divisive. God's word is divisive to our own heart and soul. God himself divides our inner being with his revelation (Heb 4:12). He offends us with his wisdom.

First Corinthians 1:18–31 tells a beautiful story of divine wisdom. At the center of that wisdom is Christ crucified. The death of Jesus is folly to a world perishing in its own pride. That Jesus would lay down his life as a ransom for the lost is folly to people who don't think themselves lost. Yet God's wisdom is salvation to those who would believe. It sometimes tells us things we don't want to hear: That we are sinners; that we are helpless to save ourselves; that we are lost apart from the grace of God. Whether we

2. See, Wilson, *Gospel According to Satan.*

3. For a good treatment of these kinds of assertions see, Wittmer, *Urban Legends of Theology.*

like it or not, God's wisdom is life-giving and life-changing. So next time God speaks to us through his word, through his Spirit, or through some annoying guy at church who happens to be right, even though we can't stand his advice and his obnoxious way of delivering it, we need to ready our hearts to listen.

STUDY QUESTIONS

1. Are there things you've believed about God that turned out to be inaccurate? How has God corrected your wrong or incomplete views?

2. Read Acts 6:1–7:60. Who is Stephen? What characterized his ministry?

3. How did he get himself into trouble with the religious authorities? What do you think Moses and the temple represent to the Jews? How might Stephen's preaching of Christ challenge conventional views of the role of Moses and the temple?

4. In what ways do you suppose the Jewish authorities missed God in their symbols, customs, and traditions?

5. How might Christians be missing God today? In other word, what correctives to our theological assumptions are needed today?

6. How do you think Stephen's death affected the hope and faith of the early church?

7. The religious and civil authorities of Stephen's day likely believed they were acting wisely and obediently. How can we know that we are following the wisdom of God and not our own ideas?

8. Read 1 Corinthians 1:18–31. How is the folly of the cross changing your life?

17

Damnation in Flame — Revelation 20

And a great sign appeared in heaven: a woman clothed with the sun, with the moon under her feet, and on her head a crown of twelve stars. She was pregnant and was crying out in birth pains and the agony of giving birth. And another sign appeared in heaven: behold, a great red dragon, with seven heads and ten horns, and on his heads seven diadems. His tail swept down a third of the stars of heaven and cast them to the earth. And the dragon stood before the woman who was about to give birth, so that when she bore her child he might devour it. She gave birth to a male child, one who is to rule all the nations with a rod of iron, but her child was caught up to God and to his throne, and the woman fled into the wilderness, where she has a place prepared by God, in which she is to be nourished for 1,260 days. Now war arose in heaven, Michael and his angels fighting against the dragon. And the dragon and his angels fought back, but he was defeated, and there was no longer any place for them in heaven. And the great dragon was thrown down, that ancient serpent, who is called the devil and Satan, the deceiver of the whole world—he was thrown down to the earth, and his angels were thrown down with him. And I heard a loud voice in heaven, saying, "Now the salvation and the power and the kingdom of our God and the authority of his Christ have come, for the accuser of our brothers has been thrown down, who accuses them day and night before our God. And they have conquered him by the blood of the Lamb and by the word of their testimony, for they loved not their lives even unto death. Therefore, rejoice, O heavens and you who dwell in them! But woe to you, O earth and sea, for the devil has come down to you in great wrath, because he knows that his time is short!"

—*REVELATION 12:1–12*

And when the thousand years are ended, Satan will be released from his prison and will come out to deceive the nations that are at the four corners of the earth, Gog and Magog, to gather them for battle; their number is like the sand of the sea. And they marched up over the broad plain of the earth and surrounded the camp of the saints and the beloved city, but fire came down from heaven and consumed them, and the devil who had deceived them was thrown into the lake of fire and sulfur where the beast and the false prophet were, and they will be tormented day and night forever and ever.

—*REVELATION 20:7–10*

SATAN (THE ADVERSARY) IS the ultimate supervillain of the Bible. This fallen angel is sometimes known as the angel of light (2 Cor 11:14), the father of lies (John 8:44), the devil (1 Pet 5:8), the dragon (Rev 12:1–12), the day star (Isa 14:12),[1] and the prince of the power of the air (Eph 2:2). A power-hungry megalomaniac, he seeks every opportunity he can to deceive and murder (John 8:44). Modern imaginations paint him as a horned goat-man with a pointy beard, wearing a red leotard and carrying a pitchfork. Dressed as a college mascot, the devil is skilled at dunking basketballs and performing sundry acrobatics. He sometimes sits on our shoulder whispering bad ideas into waiting ears, trying to inspire "fun" against our better judgment. At least that would be the cartoon version of Satan. The horror movie version of Satan is much more sinister: Rot, darkness, blood, and revulsion. This would be the Satan of the *Exorcist*—the Satan who would give *John Constantine* a run for his money.

The Bible actual never really gives us a clear description of what the devil looks like. All we know is that he's a powerful spiritual being who seems to have once held a place of prominence among God's angels. His appearance isn't relevant. Scripture is more interested in identifying him

---

1. Or, morning star.

by his actions. Satan spends most of his time tormenting followers of Jesus, leading people astray, lying, destroying, making general mischief, and plotting hairbrained schemes to usurp the throne of God so he can take over the universe.

Similar to a typical cartoon villain, Satan's schemes will never ultimately work. Revelation 12 tells us Satan got into a brawl with the archangel Michael, who body slammed his ugly devil face right out of heaven. Then God's holy warrior roundhouse kicked Satan, Chuck Norris style, and crotch-punched him so hard that a rift was torn in the fabric of the universe. The devil slunk away to wreak havoc elsewhere. He now roams the earth promoting evil, wickedness, rebellion, and dry, flavorless gluten-free products.

Revelation 12 tells us Satan has dedicated himself to battling a foe known as "the woman." So, who is this woman? Well, she's a total babe. I can tell you that much. Crowned in stars, and clothed in the sun, she stands in the heavens with the moon beneath her feet. These are all symbols of her God-given glory, authority, and divine purpose. The most natural reading of the text suggests that the woman is an allegorical representation of God's chosen people by whom his messiah, Jesus Christ, would come into the world. As commentator Leon Morris notes concerning the woman of Revelation 12: "Israel is about to give birth to the Messiah."[2]

The text of Revelation reads like a medieval fairytale. Satan is a dragon. God's people are like a damsel in distress. And God is a knight in shining armor, whose armies of heaven will ultimately defeat the dragon and restore creation from its fallen condition. We all know that dragons love damsels. Satan is no different. Whether he's targeting Eve, Mary, or the bride of Christ (the church), he is relentless. Eve, the first woman, encountered the dragon in the Garden of Eden, where he lied to her and Adam, tempting them to rebel against God and initiate the fall of humanity (Gen 3). Ever since then, Eve's progeny have been on the receiving end of the devil's schemes. Mary, who bore Israel's Messiah, later met the dragon as he unleased his human minions (namely Herod) to destroy the Christ child in Bethlehem and prevent his eventual atoning work at the cross (Matt 2:16–8). The bride of Christ, the church, faces the dragon when false teaching, dissension, disunity, and sin appear among God's people (Eph 4–6). Every time "the woman" encounters trouble, you can be sure the devil is lurking somewhere nearby.

2. Morris, *Revelation*, 153.

Satan is a jerk. But you knew that already. The question is, what does God plan to do about it? Revelation 20 answers that question. The devil will be judged eternally, consciously, and severely in the lake of fire and sulfur. In the words of the Christian thrash metal band *Stryper*, "To hell with the devil." So, let's talk about hell.

HELL IS REAL

Contrary to popular opinion, hell is not a dark fiery cave filled with devils who torture you at random—stabbing you with pitchforks and making you sit on hot coals while they laugh and jeer. Hell is not a place where people are forced to perform meaningless tasks, like digging holes, building monoliths, and rolling boulders up hills for eternity. I don't see anything in Scripture to suggest that hellish torment involves being dismembered and sewn back together, boiled in a pot as fiend stew, or eaten by gremlins. Though one should appreciate the creativity of Jan van Eyck, Hieronymus Bosch, and other Medieval artists, their repulsive yet fascinating representations of the netherworld don't fully capture the true horrors of hell.

Eternal punishment is nothing to celebrate. Few people would wish hell on anyone. The idea of hell makes us cringe to the point where we might sympathize with the words of theologian, John Frame, in his systematic theology:

> If I were free to invent my own religion, I can assure you that eternal punishment would not be part of it. But . . . I am not free to invent my own religion; I must teach only what the Bible teaches, and the Bible certainly has a lot to say about eternal punishment.[3]

Frame is right. We may not want to talk about it, but we can't simply explain it away or ignore it. Hell shows up in Scripture a lot (Mat 25:41, 46; Heb 9:27; 10:26–27, Rev 14:11; 20:10). We have to deal with it.

The Bible says Satan and the reprobate (unsaved) masses will dwell in "the lake of fire and sulfur"—a swirling vortex of agony. The true horror of hell: Those who end up there experience the full effects of the wrath of God against sin. By rejecting Jesus, who bore the wrath of God on our behalf, we are in essence inviting that same wrath on ourselves. Those who find themselves in hell are there because of their rejection of God. People aren't in hell because of ignorance, but because of rebellion against the living God.

---

3. Frame, *Systematic Theology*, 1081.

It's hard to say exactly what hell is. But this is certain: It was established by God according to his divine wisdom and inscrutable understanding. This means Satan is not the lord of hell. He's a tenant.

But you'd think the devil, who knows the Scriptures, as evidenced by his misquotation of them to Jesus in the wilderness, would know what's coming (Matt 4:1–11). You'd think he would back off a little and humbly accept his defeat. After all, the text of Revelation 20:9 is written in past tense.[4] Fire *came* down and consumed him. He was *thrown* into the lake of fire. Satan's defeat is as sure as if it already happened. But Satan is a deceiver. This means he will happily drag unsuspecting hordes to hell with him. As with many rebellious human beings, he's happy to go out shaking his fist at God. This is what we should expect from a guy who has stood in the presence of the glory and perfection of God and still doesn't give a crap about anything. That's arrogance at its fullest.

Arrogance in the face of God is what will lead Satan and "the nations" to gather against the armies of heaven in the last battle. We don't know when this battle will take place, but we do know that before the end, Satan will stage a spectacular apostasy against the Lord. Revelation 20 states that rebellious people, in their corruption and defiance of Jesus, will march against the creator and savior of the world. If you're picturing an epic, cosmic battle with edge of your seat action and peril, where the underdog good guys fight with everything they have and pull off an unlikely last second victory in true *Lord of the Rings* style, think again.

In reality, the final battle between good and evil wouldn't make for good cinema. It's all kind of anticlimactic. Jesus shows up, takes one look at Satan and his massive armies of henchmen, and basically says, "Whatever dude." Then he smashes them to a bloody pulp by sending a crazy over-the-top heavenly fireball to obliterate them. The whole thing is over in a microsecond. Smoldering goo and charred corpses will litter the earth. By the time everyone realizes what hit them, they'll all wake up swimming in the lake of fire where they get to spend eternity reflecting on what a bad idea it is to defy the Lord of the universe. Don't mess with Jesus.

GOD IS REAL TOO

By now, you will have picked up on my not-so-subtle suggestion that hell *actually* exists—an increasingly unpopular view among many contemporary

4. Morris, *Revelation*, 232.

Christians. It's become rather commonplace these days to attenuate the force of God's judgment of evil. Many professing Christians are uncomfortable talking about hell. They ignore it. They redefine it. Sometimes they deny it completely. For example, the unbiblical doctrine of universalism teaches that everyone will be saved in the end. No one has to go to hell because the loving laidback hippie Jesus will show up and make sure everyone gets saved. Similarly, the unbiblical doctrine of annihilationism is appealing to many because it allows God to still be the judge (kind of), without people having to experience justice. Annihilationism says that when sinners die, they don't have to face eternity in hell. They just kind of disappear into oblivion, more or less. That would be nice, but that's not what the Bible says.

Hell is repulsive to modern sensibilities because we don't like the fact that God is holy and that we are sinners. We diminish hell because we diminish God.[5] We think that God can't be that good, and humans can't be that bad. Consequently, if God isn't all that pure, and we're not all that dirty, then why the hell do we need the doctrine of hell? When neither God's holiness nor our sin are a big deal, then hell seems like an excessive and over-the-top judgment. When we fail to appreciate the holiness of God, we can easily end up picturing God as a bloodthirsty tyrant, cruelly trampling on the carcasses of innocent people. God becomes a bully and the punishment doesn't fit the crime. An eternity of conscious punishment all because I broke a few rules? Come on. Not fair.

The final judgment of Satan and those who follow him isn't so odd once we come to understand who God is. Because God is eternally holy, eternally loving, eternally good, and eternally just (among other things), infractions against his eternal nature carry eternal implications. All sin against an eternal God becomes eternally important. As Frame notes: "Each sin is an affront to the dignity of the eternal God, a violation of his perfect righteousness, a betrayal of his perfect love."[6] The good news is that Jesus carried the eternal weight of sin at the cross and was judged in our place. When we deny hell, we deny the weight of what Jesus did for us on the cross. But by faith in Jesus Christ and by receiving his gracious gift of life, we need not fear the horrors of hell. Heaven awaits the redeemed!

---

5. See Williams, "The Justice of Hell?"
6. Frame, *Systematic Theology*, 1083.

STUDY QUESTIONS

1. Think of a time when you didn't learn your lesson the first time, and you ended up making the same mistake twice. Revelation 12 and 20 tell us of Satan's two-fold attempt at defeating the armies of heaven.

2. Read Revelation 12:1–12. Take some time to identify all the characters in this story. Who are they and how do they relate to each other? What about the other objects and symbols in the story: What are they describing? As you ponder the woman and her child, what event from history do you think this passage is referencing?

3. What names are used in reference to the enemy of God in these verses?

4. Can you think of other moments in Scripture where there is confrontation between the "woman" and the "dragon"?

5. In what ways might the death, resurrection, and ascension of Jesus affect the devil and his power?

6. Read Revelation 20:7–10. How does God's interaction with Satan in these verses compare to his interaction with Satan in chapter 12?

7. Where do these two accounts fit chronologically, and in history past, present, and future?

8. What is Satan's ultimate fate? Did he learn his lesson from the first time he messed with God?

9. How might a follower of Jesus Christ be encouraged by these passages? Does knowing Satan's fate change how you live in and interact with the world around you?

18

Blood-Soaked Crucifix — Matthew 27, Mark 15, Luke 23, and John 19

Then Pilate took Jesus and flogged him. And the soldiers twisted together a crown of thorns and put it on his head and arrayed him in a purple robe. They came up to him, saying, "Hail, King of the Jews!" and struck him with their hands. Pilate went out again and said to them, "See, I am bringing him out to you that you may know that I find no guilt in him." So Jesus came out, wearing the crown of thorns and the purple robe. Pilate said to them, "Behold the man!" When the chief priests and the officers saw him, they cried out, "Crucify him, crucify him!" Pilate said to them, "Take him yourselves and crucify him, for I find no guilt in him." The Jews answered him, "We have a law, and according to that law he ought to die because he has made himself the Son of God." When Pilate heard this statement, he was even more afraid. He entered his headquarters again and said to Jesus, "Where are you from?" But Jesus gave him no answer. So Pilate said to him, "You will not speak to me? Do you not know that I have authority to release you and authority to crucify you?" Jesus answered him, "You would have no authority over me at all unless it had been given you from above. Therefore he who delivered me over to you has the greater sin.

From then on Pilate sought to release him, but the Jews cried out, "If you release this man, you are not Caesar's friend. Everyone who makes himself a king opposes Caesar." So when Pilate heard these words, he brought Jesus out and sat down on the judgment seat at a place called The Stone Pavement, and in

Aramaic Gabbatha. Now it was the day of Preparation of the Passover. It was about the sixth hour. He said to the Jews, "Behold your King!" They cried out, "Away with him, away with him, crucify him!" Pilate said to them, "Shall I crucify your King?" The chief priests answered, "We have no king but Caesar." So he delivered him over to them to be crucified.

—JOHN 19:1–16

MY FIRST VISUAL OF a crucifixion was thanks to the 1982 film, *Conan the Barbarian*, starring Arnold Schwarzenegger and James Earl Jones. Captured by the evil Thulsa Doom, poor Conan was sentenced to suffer on the infamous "tree of woe." Villains beware, however. Conan is hard to kill. Not even crucifixion could stop him. He merely laughed in the face of death as he hung on the cross. He then proceeded to bite the heads off every vulture and carrion bird that dared perch too close. Conan survived the crucifixion, much to the chagrin of his enemies. He went on to pretty much kill everybody in Hyboria by hacking them to pieces with a broadsword and leaving piles of bodies and heaps of gore in his wake.

Conan aside, crucifixion is one of the most brutal forms of execution invented by human beings. Of course, there were plenty of creative ancient and medieval classics that rivaled it.[1] There was the good old "breaking wheel" which was rolled over a victim's limbs or secured to the victim to break bones and cause agony. Then there was the guillotine—a clean death. The brazen bull—a scorching death. And the iron maiden, (whose actual historical use is somewhat questionable). Being drawn and quartered, hanged, whipped, stoned, or flayed would have been miserable as well. Some offenders were burned at the stake. Others were drowned. Apparently, the ancient Persians practiced a form of execution in which a victim was fastened to a small boat and fed milk and honey to attract insects who would eventually eat the victim alive.

Painful execution is generally reserved for the worst of the bad—traitors, murderers, rapists, rebels, thieves, and Galilean teachers who heal the sick and spread a message of love and hope. Jesus was killed slowly and painfully for the offense of being God and bringing salvation to the people he created. The religious and political leaders of his day saw him as a threat. Two questions naturally arise from the gospel accounts of Jesus death: 1)

1. Andrews, *Medieval Punishments*.

what was the crucifixion of Jesus like, and 2) what did the crucifixion of Jesus accomplish?

WHAT CRUCIFIXION IS

In his classic work, *The Cross of Christ*, John Stott notes that crucifixion was "probably the most cruel method of execution ever practiced, for it deliberately delayed death until maximum torture had been inflicted."[2] The Romans reserved crucifixion for the very worst murderous and treacherous non-citizen scum of their vast empire. Crucifixion was such a distasteful mode of execution that, according to commentator Leon Morris, ancient writers refused to dwell on the matter.[3] Likewise, biblical writers avoided any detail regarding Jesus' crucifixion. We're pretty much just told that "they crucified him." The gory details have largely been left to *The Passion of the Christ* and other Hollywood productions of the life and death of Jesus.

Our best historical and scientific explanation of the crucifixion process comes from an article entitled, "On the Physical Death of Jesus Christ," written by three medical doctors, and published in the *Journal of the American Medical Association*.[4] What follows has been lifted from that text and summarized here for your shock, horror, and education.

Crucifixion is a precise artform—each step in the process designed to maximize pain. Jesus was first scourged with whips that would likely have included fragments of animal bone, metal, or other sharp objects. The purpose of the whip was to tear and lacerate the skin, leaving it in ribbons. John 19:2 recounts that a crown of thorns was pressed into Jesus' scalp. A purple robe was then placed on his back. This was intended as mockery—psychological torture. The cloth of the purple robe would no doubt have stuck to the drying, coagulating blood making its removal a painful ordeal.

John's account has Jesus led out of the city bearing the patibulum, or cross beam, to which he would eventually be nailed. The half-mile journey to the Place of the Skull no doubt weakened Jesus with each step until his strength finally gave out. This is why the synoptic gospels cite that a man called Simon of Cyrene was conscripted by the Romans to bear the patibulum in Jesus' stead.

---

2. Stott, *Cross of Christ*, 31.

3. Morris, *Gospel According to Matthew*, 708.

4. Edwards et al., "Physical Death of Jesus Christ," 1455–63.

Having arrived at the Place of the Skull, where Jesus' crucifixion would take place, he was thrown down on the rough-hewn beam. As splinters dug into his shredded back, his arms were stretched out over the patibulum. Iron spikes, approximately six inches in length, were driven into his wrists to secure him to the beam, inflicting excruciating pain as flesh, bone, and nerves were torn and severed.

The patibulum was then raised and fixed to the upright wooden pole. From there, the feet were attached to the pole with a third and final nail through the arches of the feet to ensure that the knees remained painfully flexed. Once Jesus had been secured to the cross, the slow, agonizing wait began.

The true torment of crucifixion was not from loss of blood, but from slow asphyxiation. As the hours passed, Jesus' beaten and weakened body was unable to support itself. Each breath became more and more belabored. Exhalation became nearly impossible. Flies and other insects landed in the wounds, burrowing and biting. Scavenger birds waited to feed on dying flesh. With each breath, the lacerated back of the Christ painfully rubbed the splinters of the wooden pole. Loss of strength and loss of oxygen took their toll until Jesus uttered his final word, breathed his final breath, and gave up his spirit. Dehydration, heart failure, suffocation, trauma to muscles, skin and nerves converged to make the death an excruciating event.

Jesus' physical agony was coupled with emotional agony. His people had rejected him. One of his disciples had betrayed him. Another had denied him. The rest had fled. It seems only John dared return at some point during those long hours to gaze on and grieve his dying friend (John 19:25–27). The feelings of abandonment would have been visceral and tragic.

In addition to physical and emotional suffering, the spiritual suffering of Jesus took his agony to another level—a level unknown to anyone else in history. The perfect Son of God, the creator of the world, the sinless Lord had been subjected to the sin of the world. Though innocent, he bore our deserved wounds. Though perfect, he bore our imperfections. Though absolute in holiness, he bore the consequences of our rebellion and paid the debt we owed him with his own blood (Isa 53).

WHAT CHRIST'S CRUCIFIXION DOES

So, Jesus died a horrible death. A lot of people die horrible deaths. So what? Jesus suffered. A lot of people suffer. What's the big deal?

This: The death of Jesus is unique in that Jesus uniquely accomplished atonement for sin and salvation for sinners. His death is unique in that he is unique. Jesus is truly God and truly man, making him unlike any other person who ever lived. As a man, Jesus was able to represent human beings and bear the sins of human beings. As God, Jesus lived a sinless life and demonstrated the fullness of God's love, mercy, grace, holiness, justice, and wrath by laying down his life in our place.

The heart of the gospel is the atonement—the sacrificial death and glorious resurrection of Jesus. It's that simple. This is the message announced by angels: "He will save his people from their sins" (Mat 1:21). This is the message declared by John the Baptist: "Behold the Lamb of God, who takes away the sin of the world" (John 1:29). This is the message preached by Peter at Pentecost: "Repent and be baptized every one of you in the name of Jesus Christ for the forgiveness of your sins" (Acts 2:38). This is the message that Paul preached again and again: That Jesus gave himself for our sins to deliver us from the present evil age (Gal 1:4). Jesus himself preached this message when he said that God had given his one and only Son, to lay his life down for his people (John 3:16; 10:15, 18).

Our hope is rooted in substitutionary atonement—the events surrounding the crucifixion of Christ. Despite this fact, I hear murmurings within the Protestant Christian world that the cross alone makes for an anemic gospel. More is needed, I'm told. Some want a bigger gospel, a fuller gospel. The "real" gospel, I'm told, is about being with Jesus and doing *Jesusee* kinds of things. The "real" gospel, I'm told, exists to generate justice seekers, kingdom citizens, and activists. I'm told the "real," more complete, more relevant, more transformative gospel is *more* about the kingship of Jesus, and *less* about his cross. Sure, the cross is important, but it's a byproduct of the "real" gospel where Jesus shows us how to usher in social change and fix the problems of hurting people.

I'm told the cross isn't enough. I disagree. Now, we should heartily affirm that Jesus came to inaugurate a kingdom of justice that will be fully realized at his future return (Luke 4:16–20). We should happily assert that the fruit of the gospel is transformation of individuals, families, communities, and societies. We should readily defend the kingship and lordship of Jesus as declared throughout the pages of Scripture. But there's a problem with the "real" gospel outlined above: It gets things out of order and relegates the cross to a secondary status.

If the gospel is reduced to following Jesus' example and doing *Jesusee* kinds of things, I'm not convinced that's good enough news to make it *the* good news. Sure, Jesus was a great teacher and compassionate healer. But there are plenty of other wise gurus and justice-oriented philosophers to follow on social media. Is Jesus a better spiritual advisor than Plato, Aristotle, Marcus Aurelias, Buddha, Gandhi, Mother Theressa, or Oprah? Why should anyone care about being uniquely like Jesus unless Jesus did something uniquely worthy of our devotion? This is why the cross is not secondary.[5] Without the atoning work of Jesus at the cross, there's nothing in the story of Jesus' life that couldn't have been done by someone else.

If we turn the gospel into something humans can do apart from God (e.g. practicing generosity and kindness and seeking the common good of those around us), or something God can do apart from Christ (e.g. announcing a kingdom ethic and calling people to obedience to God), then we've lost sight of why Christ came. Only Jesus Christ could do what Jesus Christ did at the cross—achieve the forgiveness of sin once for all. Greg Gilbert states:

> Scripture makes it clear that the cross must remain at the center of the gospel. We cannot move it to the side, and we cannot replace it with any other truth as the heart, center, and foundation of the good news. To do so is to present the world with something that is not saving, and that is therefore not good news at all.[6]

The world wants a Christianity that keeps to itself while reinforcing the status quo and providing some social benefit to its citizens. But we preach Christ crucified, a stumbling block and offense (1 Cor 1:23). The world is happy enough with a gospel that offers mere self-improvement. But we preach that humans are great sinners, and that Jesus is a greater savior.

The death of Jesus accomplishes several things:

Restoration for sinners and sufferers—All of us suffer in this life as a result of the fallen human condition. When our first parents Adam and Eve rebelled against God, they invited sin, sickness, and death into the world (Rom 5:12). God, however, has not left us to endure our fallen condition alone. He came to live, suffer, and die as a human among humans. Before we blame God for all the evils we see in the world, we must remember all the evils we have committed against God—we deny him, accuse him, doubt

---

5. For an excellent treatment of the biblical gospel, with mention of deviant views, see Gilbert, *What is the Gosepl?*

6. Gilbert, *What is the Gospel,* 110.

him, break his laws, and harm his creation. We perpetually reject him. But despite this rejection, he has not withdrawn from us. On the contrary, he pursues the lost and broken. The cross of Christ is where we bring our brokenness and sin. We deliver our fallenness to Jesus, who receives it, and offers us an eternal solution in return. John Stott put it perfectly:

> I could never myself believe in God, if it were not for the cross. The only God I believe in is the one Nietzsche ridiculed as 'God on the cross.' In the real world of pain, how could one worship a God who was immune to it? I have entered many Buddhist temples in different Asian countries and stood respectfully before the statue of the Buddha, his legs crossed, arms folded, eyes closed, the ghost of a smile playing round his mouth, a remote look on his face, detached from the agonies of the world. But each time after a while I have had to turn away. And in imagination I have turned instead to that lonely, twisted, tortured figure on the cross, nails through hands and feet, back lacerated, limbs wrenched, brow bleeding from thorn-pricks, mouth dry and intolerably thirsty, plunged in Godforsaken darkness. That is the God for me! He laid aside his immunity to pain. He entered our world of flesh and blood, tears and death. He suffered for us.[7]

The cross of Jesus Christ is a demonstration of God's tenderness, mercy, and grace. Jesus did what no other mystic, sage, or guru has ever achieved.

Fulfillment of prophecy—From before the foundation of the world was laid, God had established a solution to the problems we would create (Eph 1:4). Even as our first parents fell into spiritual death in the garden, God made a promise. The offspring of the woman, Eve, would crush the head of the dragon, Satan (Gen 3:15). Later, God Promised Abraham that through his offspring (namely Jesus) the nations would be blessed (Gen 12:1–3). God renewed this promise by telling David that one of his descendants (Jesus again) would reign forever on his throne (2 Sam 7:12–6). The Old Testament prepares us for Jesus. The New Testament explains what the Old Testament prepared us for. In essence, the whole of the Bible is about Jesus, and his cross. Without it, the story falls flat, humans are doomed, and there is no hope.

Punishment for sin and redemption for sinners—Sin cannot go unpunished. Any judge who lets a criminal go is unjust. Any criminal who fails to confess and pay is guilty of more than their original crime. We desire justice. We expect justice. We require justice. In Jesus, justice was served.

7. Stott, *Cross of Christ*, 387.

By taking the sins of the elect on himself, Jesus bore God's wrath against sin and served as the propitiation, or appeasement, for sin. Every lash, every cut, every strike, every insult, rejection, and denial was deserved (deserved by us; paid by him). By going to the Father on behalf of the fallen, Jesus served as the expiation, or atoning reparation. Jesus fulfilled the sacrificial system of the Old Testament by doing what bulls, sheep, and goats could never accomplish (Lev 16). Sin was imputed to him. In turn, salvation was imputed to those who would put their confidence in him and him alone. Jesus saved us from our sin. Jesus also saved us from the wrath of God.

All the violent deaths committed by humans and against humans culminate at the cross. No violent death in the Bible carries greater weight and accomplished more than the death of Jesus Christ. His precious death and glorious resurrection are the point of it all. The glorification of God by Jesus' work at the cross are central to all time and space. If anyone would like to know God's love, then look at the cross. If anyone would like to know God's holiness, look again at the cross. The cross is where we see the breadth of God's attributes converge on full display. Look at the cross. But don't just look. Praise the Christ who died. Confess your sin. Receive his love and forgiveness. There's salvation at the foot of the cross.

STUDY QUESTIONS

1. Have you ever been wrongly accused?

2. Read John 19:1–16. Summarize the events of these verses in your own words. Who are the main characters? Where are they? What are they doing?

3. Note the different ways Jesus suffered in the text. Was Jesus suffering purely physical?

4. What was Jesus' crime? Jesus is said to be the Son of God. In what way is this considered a crime in the minds of the chief priests and leaders? How do we accuse and reject God today?

5. Describe Pilate's behavior. What is going on in his mind? What kind of leader is he?

6. Describe the behavior of the chief priests and other leaders. What do you think is motivating their vitriol?

7. Can you relate in any ways to Pilate and the Jewish leaders? Explain.

8. Who is Jesus and what did his crucifixion accomplish? See Ephesians 2:1–10 and Isaiah 52:13–53:12.

9. Where do we see both judgment and redemption in the event of the crucifixion of Jesus?

10. What should the cross of Christ change in you?

Bibliography

Allbright, William F. *Archaeology and the Religion of Israel*. Baltimore: Johns Hopkins Press, 1942.

Andrews, William. *Medieval Punishments: An Illustrated History of Torture*. New York: Skyhorse, 2013.

Bainton, Ronald H. *Here I Stand: A Life of Martin Luther*. Nashville, TN: Abingdon, 1950.

Bejon, James "Judas's Demise in Matthew 27 and Acts 1: Do They Contradict?" https://www.thegospelcoalition.org/article/judas-demise-matthew-1-acts-1/.

Beza, Theodore. "*The Life of John Calvin.*" In *Selected Works of John Calvin*, Vol. 1, edited by H. Beveridge and J. Bonnet. Grand Rapids, MI: Baker, 1983.

Boghossian, Peter. *A Manual for Creating Atheists*. Durham, NC: Pitchstone, 2013.

Carson, D.A. *The Difficult Doctrine of the Love of God*. Wheaton IL: Crossway, 2000.

Carson, D.A. ed. *The Enduring Authority of the Christian Scriptures*. Grand Rapids, MI: Wm. B. Eerdmans, 2016.

Chan, Francis. *The Forgotten God: Reversing Our Tragic Neglect of the Holy Spirit*. Colorado Springs, CO: David C. Cook, 2009.

Childers, Alisa. *Live Your Truth and Other Lies: Exposing Popular Deceptions that Make Us Anxious, Exhausted, and Self-Obsessed*. Carol Stream, IL: Tyndale Momentum, 2022.

Copan, Paul. *Is God a Moral Monster: Making Sense of the Old Testament God*. Grand Rapids, MI: Baker, 2011.

Craig, William Lane, and J.P. Moreland. *Philosophical Foundations for a Christian Worldview*. Downers Grove, IL: InterVarsity, 2003.

Cundall, Arthur E. *Judges*, Tyndale Old Testament Commentaries. London: Tyndale, 1968.

Dante Alighieri. *The Divine Comedy: Inferno*. Various Translations.

Davis, Dale Ralph. *Judges: Such a Great Salvation*. Focus on the Bible Commentary. Fearn, UK: Christian Focus, 2000.

———. *1 Kings: The Wisdom and the Folly*. Focus on the Bible Commentary. Fearn, UK: Christian Focus, 2002.

———. *2 Kings: The Power and the Fury*. Focus on the Bible Commentary. Fearn, UK: Christian Focus, 2005.

Day, John. *Molech: A God of Human Sacrifice in the Old Testament*. New York: Cambridge University Press, 1989.

Dawkins, Richard. *The God Delusion*. Boston: Houghton Mifflin, 2006.

Edwards, William D., Wesley J. Gabel, and Floyd E. Hosmer, "On the Physical Death of Jesus Christ," *Journal of the American Medical Association*, 225.11 (1986) 1455–63.

Enns, Peter. *The Bible Tells Me So: Why Defending Scripture Has Made Us Unable to Read It.* New York: HarperOne, 2014.

Flavius Josephus, *The Antiquities of the Jews.* Various Translations.

Frame, John. *The Doctrine of the Word of God.* Phillipsburg, NJ: P&R, 2010.

———. *Systematic Theology: An Introduction to Christian Belief.* Phillipsburg, NJ: P&R, 2007.

Gervais Martial Hounnou, et al. "Anatomical Study of the Length of the Human Intestine." *Surgical and Radiologic Anatomy,* 24.5 (2002) 290–4.

Gilbert, Greg. *What is the Gospel?* Wheaton, IL: Crossway, 2010.

Groothuis, Douglas. *Truth Decay: Defending Christianity Against the Challenges of Postmodernism.* Downers Grove, IL: InterVarsity, 2000.

Grossman, Cathy Lynn. "Witch Books Hold Power." https://www.publishersweekly.com/pw/by-topic/industry-news/religion/article/89917-witch-books-hold-power.html.

Grudem, Wayne A. *Systematic Theology: An Introduction to Biblical Doctrine.* 2nd ed. Grand Rapids, MI: Zondervan, 2020.

———. *Christian Beliefs: Twenty Basics Every Christian Should Know.* Revised edition. Grand Rapids, MI: Zondervan, 2022.

Henry, Matthew. "Commentary on the Whole Bible, Complete and Unabridged in One Volume." Peabody, MA: Hendrickson, 1991.

Hess, Richard S. *Joshua,* Tyndale Old Testament Commentaries. Downers Grove, IL: InterVarsity, 1996.

Jarry, Jonathan. "Are You Left-Handed? Science Still Yearns to Know Why." McGill University. https://www.mcgill.ca/oss/article/health-general-science/are-you-left-handed-science-still-yearns-know-why.

Jensen, Morten Horning. "Antipas: The Herod Jesus Knew," Biblical Archeology Review 38.5 (2012).

Keller, Timothy. *Judges for You.* Epsom, UK: The Good Book Company, 2013.

———. *Preaching: Communicating Faith in an Age of Skepticism.* New York: Viking, 2015.

Klein, Lilian R. *The Triumph of Irony in the Book of Judges.* Decatur, GA: Almond, 1989.

Knipe, David M. *Hinduism: Experiments in the Sacred.* San Francisco: Harper, 1991.

Mark, Joshua J. "The Ancient City," *World History Encyclopedia,* https://www.worldhistory.org/city/, 2014.

Morris, Leon. *The Gospel According to Matthew,* Pillar New Testament Commentary. Grand Rapids, MI: Eerdmans, 1995.

———. *Revelation,* The Tyndale New Testament Commentaries, 2nd ed. Grand Rapids, MI: William B. Eerdmans, 1987.

Myers, John Myers. *The Saga of Hugh Glass: Pirate, Pawnee, and Mountain Man.* Lincoln, NE: Bison, 1976.

Patai, Raphael. *Sex and Marriage in the Bible and the Middle East.* Garden City, NJ: Doubleday, 1959.

Perozzi, Christina and Hallie Beaune, *The Naked Pint: An Unadulterated Guide to Craft Beer.* New York: Pedigree, 2009.

Rabinovitch, Shelley and James Lewis, *The Encyclopedia of Modern Witchcraft and Neo-Paganism.* New York: Citadel, 2002.

Smith III, Joseph W. *Sex and Violence in the Bible: A Survey of Explicit Content in the Holy Book.* Phillipsburg, NJ: P&R, 2014.

Sproul, R.C. *Acts: An Expositional Commentary.* Sanford, FL: Ligonier Ministries, 2019.

———. *The Holiness of God.* Wheaton, IL: Tyndale, 1985.

Stott, John. *The Cross of Christ*. 20th Anniversary Edition. Downers Grove, IL: InterVarsity, 2006.

Wedgwood, C.V. *The Thirty Years War*. London: J. Cape, 1938.

Wessel, Walter W. *Mark*, Expositors Bible Commentary. Volume 8, ed. Frank E. Gaebelein. Grand Rapids: Regency, 1984.

Williams, Donald T. "The Justice of Hell?", *Christian Research Journal*, (2017) (Updated June 29, 2023). https://www.equip.org/articles/the-justice-of-hell/.

Wilson, Jared C. *The Gospel According to Satan: Eight Lies About God that Sound Like the Truth*. Nashville: Nelson Books, 2020.

Wittmer, Michael. *Urban Legends of Theology: 40 Misconceptions*. Brentwood, TN: B&H Academic, 2023.

Scripture Index